# PO SHUN LEONG

## MAKING ART BOXES

Tony Lydgate / Principal photography by Sze Lei Leong

**Sterling Publishing Co., Inc.**
New York
A STERLING/CHAPELLE BOOK

**For my wife Poh Suan and sons, Sze Tsung and Sze Lei.**

Chapelle Ltd.
Owner: Jo Packham

Text and coordination: Tony Lydgate
Graphic design: Sze Tsung Leong
Principal photographer: Sze Lei Leong
Additional photos: Timothy Lydgate, John Adams, Michel Zabé
Technical drawings: Richard Long

Library of Congress Cataloging-in-Publication Data Available

10 9 8 7 6 5 4 3 2 1

A STERLING / CHAPELLE BOOK

Published 2001 by Sterling Publishing Company, Inc.
387 Park Avenue South, New York, N.Y. 10016
Originally published by Sterling Publishing as *Art Boxes*
© 1998 by Po Shun Leong and Chapelle Ltd.
Distributed in Canada by Sterling Publishing
%Canadian Manda Group, One Atlantic Avenue, Suite 105
Toronto, Ontario, Canada M6K 3E7
Distributed in Great Britain and Europe by Cassell PLC
Wellington House, 125 Strand, London WC2R 0BB, England
Distributed in Australia by Capricorn Link (Australia) Pty Ltd.
P.O. Box 6651, Baulkham Hills, Business Centre, NSW 2153, Australia
*Printed in China*
*All rights reserved*

Sterling ISBN 0-8069-7955-0

Every effort has been made to ensure that all of the information in this book is accurate. However, due to differing conditions, tools, and individual skills, the publisher cannot be responsible for any injuries, losses, and/or other damages which may result from the use of information in this book.

If you have any questions or comments or would like information about any specialty products featured in this book, please contact:
Chapelle Ltd., Inc., P.O. BOX 9252, Ogden, UT 84409.
Tel (801) 621-2777, fax (801) 621-2788.

Cover photo: *Landscape Box*, 1997. Cherry Burl Front. 24"h x 21"w x 9"d.
Page 1: *Figure*, 1993, detail.
Previous page: *In Construction*, 1995. Detail. Bleached wenge. 15"h x 9"w x 8"d.
Opposite page: *Industrial*, 1990. Wood collage. 17¼" x 17¼".

# CONTENTS

This is a book about some of the most extraordinary boxes ever made.

Despite their intricate appearance, they were all built using only the most basic woodworking tools and techniques, which are presented in detail in "Creating Art Boxes," a special sixty-eight page section beginning on page 58.

This step-by-step guide gives complete how-to instructions, and includes five projects specially designed for woodworkers of any skill level, from beginner to expert.

# PO SHUN LEONG

Born in England, where his parents had emigrated from China, Po Shun was sent to the countryside to live with family friends for safety during the closing years of the Second World War. In the dining room of the home where he stayed was a huge wooden model of an ocean liner, complete in every detail. Using marbles as passengers, the boy played with this model for hours at a time, exploring the intricate arrangement of cabins, decks and passageways, and imagining what it might feel like actually to be inside such a complex design.

Imagination, complexity, enjoyment, and a sense of wonder are some of the many elements woven into Po Shun's art boxes. Gathered together for the first time in this book, this remarkable body of woodwork evokes a powerful sense of visual excitement and drama, inviting the viewer of each piece to embark on a voyage of exploration, discovery and surprise.

Above: *Day of the Dead*, 1967.

An interest in designing and building environments that respond to people's practical and aesthetic needs led Po Shun to a degree from the Architectural Association School in London, from which he graduated in 1964. He was awarded a fellowship to study

in France with the architect Charles-Edouard Jeanneret, better known as Le Corbusier, and lived at La Tourette, the master's recently built Dominican Monastery near Lyons. As part of his education, Po Shun was able to travel widely, studying the buildings of ancient Rome, Italy and Greece, the cities and cathedrals of Europe, and the modern architecture rising throughout the continent.

Po Shun practiced architecture in London for a brief period, but his interest in human welfare soon led him to volunteer to work in Mexico with the American Friends Service Committee. In 1966 he was sent to Cuauhtenco, a rural area east of Mexico City. The greatest challenge for a designer in this remote region was to create appropriate architecture that could be built using indigenous labor and materials. In partnership with the Mexican Government, Po Shun used a prefabricated construction system to design a total of 27 public schools. He was also involved in designing and building bridges, wells, and water supply systems, as well as in setting up a project to market textiles woven by local residents.

Above: Le Corbusier. La Tourette Monastery, 1963.

Prefabricated schools,
Mexico, 1967.

Festival of Children's mural painting, Mexico, 1968.

Musical sculpture, 1968.

Mexico is renowned for its tradition of murals in public places, which includes works by artists such as Siquieros, Orozco, and Diego Rivera. During the 1968 Olympics in Mexico City, Po Shun was asked to coordinate an International Festival of Children's Mural Painting, involving children from all the countries participating in the Olympics. At the conclusion of the project, the murals were used to line the Paseo de la Reforma, the city's main avenue. With Po Shun as organizer, the children also constructed musical sculptures, made of colorful anodized aluminum parts, which sang as the wind energized them.

Furniture store,
Mexico City, 1974.

Po Shun went back to London briefly in 1969 to marry Poh Suan Tang, whom he had met when they were both students at the Architectural Association. Returning to Mexico City with his bride and fellow architect, for the next 15 years he fulfilled commissions to design commercial and residential buildings. At the same time, Po Shun was administering local handcrafts or artesania for the Government. To increase the number of jobs within the region's existing technology, he organized shows and exhibitions, and worked with craft makers to expand the market for artesania by creating cottage industries. In his spare time, he painted landscapes of the Mexican countryside, and of the villages where he stayed.

Architects are known for their obsession with chairs, and Po Shun is no exception. He created a number of award-winning chair designs during his years in Mexico, several of which were commercially produced for use at resort hotels along Mexico's Gulf and Pacific coasts. (Two recent chair designs appear on pages 38 and 47.)

Po Shun's interest in indigenous industry led him to design a chair in which native palm weavings, normally used to make hats, were stretched over factory-built wooden forms to make furniture parts. These parts were then used to produce living room fur-

*Fiberglass Recliner, 1972.*

*Polyurethane
Chair, 1974.*

*Mahogany Chair, 1976.*

*Palm Chairs, 1980.*

Far left: *Dining Chair*, 1982.
Left: *Rocking Chair*, 1991.

niture, of which more than ten thousand sets were sold at $50 apiece. Po Shun's efforts were recognized by a special award from the President of Mexico; he received a commission from another former President to make furniture for his residence in Acapulco.

As economic conditions in Mexico changed, Po Shun and his family, which now included two sons, decided in 1982 to move to the United States, settling in Southern California. Using his skill and experience as a furniture designer, Po Shun won several national furniture competitions, and a number of his designs were put into production.

In between building prototypes for the American furniture industry, Po Shun crafted small boxes, which he began to sell locally. The box in the photograph below, with its six swivel drawers, was designed in 1983, and produced in Po Shun's studio as a multiple. Although this functional box is simple in appearance, making it proved time-consuming, because of the amount of sanding required to produce the curved shapes and create a smooth exterior.

To solve the problem of too much sanding, Po Shun returned to his architectural roots. He began to build a series of boxes that incorporated the forms and shapes of classical design: the circle, square, and triangle, in their architectural manifestations as column and cone, arch and stair, finial and tower. These basic shapes could be cut out on the bandsaw, and then assembled with glue, avoiding the need for either sanding or time-consuming joinery and the advanced machinery to mill it.

*Cresent Box*, 1983.

Po Shun's boxes became increasingly complex and elaborate, and this new design direction proved so fruitful that it became an obsession, fueled by the pleasant sense of daily accomplishment. (Most architectural and furniture designs never get built, and the few that do not only take years, but often end up bearing scant resemblance to the designer's original concept; thus the quick, tangible results of boxmaking offered a welcome contrast.) Another contrast was the way the new work allowed the artist to be playful, even humorous. "I think I'm at my best when I'm playing," Po Shun has said. "It's important to maintain what you might call childfulness."

By incorporating symmetry in his new designs, and by framing them within simple shapes, often a rectangle or a square, Po Shun brought composure and balance to an emerging visu-

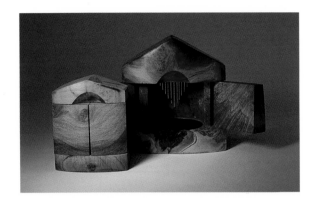

al complexity that might otherwise have seemed overwhelming. This frame also enhanced the feeling of harnessed or contained energy, of intricate life packed into the tight space of the work, which gave it drama: as the viewer explored a piece, gradually uncovering its secrets, the experience of excitement, intrigue, and anticipation was unavoidable.

As his designs evolved, Po Shun began to play with the idea of recognizability, by incorporating direct and indirect visual references to famous and legendary buildings and places, some of which are illustrated on page 61. As a result, although his boxes project an aura of mystery, there is always something strangely familiar about them.

Decades of designing for practical human needs sensitized the artist to the importance of what has come to be called user-friendliness, and he was careful to build this into each new piece. Despite their dramatic appearance, his boxes draw you in. They are inviting, rather than austere. The warm wood, the playful shapes, the multiple drawers and doors: everything says, "Please touch." Then the voyage of discovery begins. As Po Shun has written:

> The sense of surprise is important. My boxes can't be seen all at once; people keep saying, "But wait—there's more!" Then you have to keep on looking to discover the more. Wherever there's a window, you have to look through it. Wherever there's a flight of stairs, you have to climb them. Wherever there's an archway, you have to pass underneath.
>
> My boxes are not about woodwork. They're about magic and drama. I've chosen to work in wood because it's very forgiving. It offers a broad color palette, and you can use every part, especially the fissures and cracks. There are dramatic contrasts between light and dark, rough and smooth, linear and organic. It's also very immediate: you just put it there and it's done. No need to fire and glaze, as with clay.

Although wood is his principal medium, Po Shun carefully designs his pieces to avoid what he considers the drudgery of joinery. Self-taught as a woodworker, he uses only the most basic woodworking tools, techniques, and machinery. For him, like the wood itself, these are simply a means to the end all artists seek: to strike a responsive chord. The resonance Po Shun's work evokes within us is unusually powerful because it touches so many of our senses. He gives us visual, tactile, and intellectual delight, drama, and grandeur, and a sense of continuity with our human past—all conveyed in that most familiar and approachable of objects, the box.

# CONTAINMENT OF IDEAS

The Architectonic Constructions of Po Shun Leong

*Jo Lauria*

## The Importance of the Container

Po Shun Leong's wooden boxes and sculptural constructions are metaphors for containment. Rooted in art and architecture and mediated by the mythic, these constructions provoke a reading on both the visual and intellectual plane. The rich detailing and multi-layering of visible information lead the eye on an endless exploration of material space—the shell, the shelter, the container—and invite the mind to consider the mystery of the enclosed, elusive, and illusionary space. These constructions then can be contemplated as both containers of, and conduits to, the physical universe and the metaphorical universe.

The physicality of Leong's sculptural works make a tangible statement about compartmentalization; and on an intangible level, about protection, value, and preservation. Indeed, mankind has a direct linkage to the container. We enter the world directly from the womb to the containment of the cradle. Our remains are contained in the coffins, caskets, and urns, and interned in graves and mausoleums. Close examination reveals the body to be the ultimate container: the skeleton is contained by the skin, the brain is encased in the skull, and the whole body structure serves as the chamber for the soul.

A profound association with containment can readily be seen in the ancient Egyptian civilization. The monumental tomb architecture of IV and V dynasty Egypt gives form to the philosophy of sacred space and the reality of containment. The pyramids are constructed of inner sepulchral chambers that contain the revered mummified bodies of the rulers. Further, the visceral remains of the sanctified are contained in canopic jars entombed with the bodies. One first encounters, and is awed by, the outward structure of the pyramid. One must then negotiate interior passageways to gain entrance to the inner sanctum. It is an inward journey of revelation; a discovery to reveal hidden wonders, both material and spiritual.

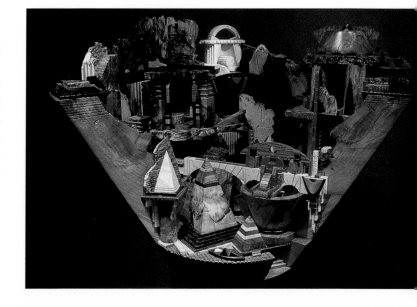

Po Shun Leong. *Pompeii Vessel*, 1990. Detail.

## The Treasure Boxes

On a smaller, more intimate and private scale, Leong's treasure boxes restate this ancient relationship to containment. The overlay of complex architectural information, the intricate design, and the concealed drawers engage the viewer on the same levels as the architectural monuments: they invite reflection and wonderment of the facade and the mystery it holds within: an illicit participation to discover and expose the interior secret compartments.

Living with a Leong treasure box is like owning a personal monument. Indeed, the inspiration for these boxes can be traced back to the centuries-old practice of building models of monuments as mementos. The scale model of Muhafiz Khan's Mosque built in 1838 as a replica of the fifteenth-century Indian mosque at Ahmedabad serves as an historical record of this tradition. The model was fabricated for a British office in the East India Company, and is similar in detail and scale to models that were made in the nineteenth-century to be taken home by European visitors as mementos of their East Indian adventure.

*Model of Muhafiz Khan's Mosque,* India, 1838.

Another intention of the "model monument" is evidenced in the miniaturized wooden buildings created by the English architect Sir John Soane. Soane's constructions were used as working models to inform the tradesmen about particular materials and techniques, and as dimensional blueprints to visualize the exterior and interior for the client. It is obvious from Soane's elaborate model of Tyringham House, Buckinghamshire, that the architect built these scaled-down monuments not only as schema but as decorative objects for display and enrichment.

The idea of the box as replicated monument is evident in all Leong's work. The emphasis is not, however, on the exact reproduction of existing architecture; it is on the creation of a mythological landscape. Leong's box constructions are architectural collages which incorporate references, direct and oblique, to legendary historical structures. The ordered and repeating columns, the pediments and friezes, reference Greco-Roman temples. The steep climbing stairs recall both the stepped face of the pyramids and the set-back zig-zag skyscrapers of the art deco era. The manner in which Leong's structures appear chiseled from monoliths evokes the mysterious architecture of such cities as ancient

*Model of Tyringham House,* England, 1795.

Petra (2000 B.C.), a rock-cut Arab city of hundreds of houses, temples, and tombs carved entirely from the imposing sandstone cliff; and Mesa Verde, the North American Anasazi canyon pueblos (1200 A.D.), "cliff dwellings," sculpted from the Colorado mountains. This melange of architectural references serves equally as an ocular device to intrigue the eye and as a framework to consider the fantastic.

Left: Drawing of Mesa Verde, Colorado, 1200 A.D.

It is clear that Leong's central strategy is the appropriation of architectural styles which function as forms of identification and classification. If one goes beyond the facade, it is apparent that Leong also appropriates structures of the treasure box. Boxes for keeping treasure were prized objects d'art of sixteenth- through eighteenth-century Asia and Europe. An exquisite wood and inlaid bone "Writing Cabinet" from India is a fine early example of a box crafted to contain treasure. In this case, the treasure refers to the valued implements of writing. The poetic verses which are written in gold along the outer border of the front door proclaim the beauty and importance of this cabinet's function:

*Writing Cabinet,* India, 1558–1559.

*I saw a jeweled chest.*
*I asked it, "What are you and what name do you bear?*

Another specialty box of note is a Chinese wood carved "Treasure Box" from the Ch'ing dynasty (1736-95). The box was specifically designed for the containment and presentation of small-scale antique replicas of miniature art and sculpture from the imperial collections of the Ch'ing Emperor. It is an ingenious three-dimensional puzzle construction of hidden drawers and concealed compartments.

A slightly different interpretation of the form can be seen in the eighteenth-century "Necessaire And Watch"

*Treasure Box,* China, 1736–1795.

executed by the British metal smith James Cox. This ornate jeweled chiming clock is comprised of two small simulated chests of drawers supported by elephants. The seemingly seamless upper chest opens to reveal a drawer containing such personal effects as a pair of tweezers, a combined ear and toothpick, scissors, a pencil, a penknife, and ivory tablets. This exotic and eccentric object is the protean treasure box as it tells time, chimes, and conceals.

Left: *Necessaire And Watch,*
London, 1766–1772.

Leong's treasure boxes are the perfect infusion of historical quotation and invention. Leong appropriates form, style and surface from oriental and occidental sources. In doing so, he allows these references in his work to function like trace elements—essential to the overall scheme but not exclusive. Leong's singular approach to design and his personal vision of the box as mythological architecture render his works fresh and original.

Naum Gabo. *Linear Construction in Space,* 1959.

## The Sculptural Constructions

Although the metaphor of containment is essential to Leong's oeuvre, the constructions which are not tied to function show a direct connection to contemporary sculpture. Leong's work is most closely aligned with Constructivism, an aesthetic launched in the early twentieth-century and associated with the sculptures and paintings of Gabo, Pevsner, Malevich, Kandinsky, and Archipenko. Constructivism as applied to sculptural concepts introduced a new vocabulary. Traditional sculpture relies on the presentation of mass in space—solid, opaque volumes usually carved or cast from one unit that fill space. Constructivist sculpture is assembled sculpture of which the most important plastic properties are planes, edges, penetrations, and profiles. Solid mass is interpolated by inner voids which establish the sculpture's depth in space.

Russian artist Naum Gabo (1890-1978) well illustrates these tenets in his 1959 "Linear Construction in Space." Leong was introduced to Gabo when Leong was a teenager living in England. Leong showed Gabo his sketches and Gabo encouraged him to continue on his study of art and architecture. Gabo's direct influence is evident in Leong's

grasp of pure constructivist principles: Leong's "Pylon" (page 26) is an assembled sculptural form constructed of intersecting planes which are penetrated by the voids so that all surfaces, inside and outside, are made visible to the viewer.

Joseph Cornell's assemblage boxes strongly influence the sculptural collages of Leong. The way in which Cornell organizes his world within the limits of the frame, wherein objects are places in a grid system and compartmentalized, is the device which Leong uses to define his compositions. The isolation of objects within confined grid boxes, and the stacking of these boxes, connote urban environments. In Cornell's "Dovecote" boxes these environments are poetic "bird habitats," the bird being the metaphor for spiritual life, and the habitat the shelter in which this life is safeguarded. In Leong's "Triptych: The Rise and Fall of the City of Mahagonny" two urban landscapes are stacked, one on top of the other. The lower level depicts archaeological life; that is, the decay and deposit of fallen civilization. A new city, renewed and vital, rises above the arc-like horizon line, an important grid line which separates the dynamic upper level from the detritus below. Though the artist has a different orientation toward content, both presentations are theatrical: they tell their story through selection, reduction, and arrangement.

## Sum of the Parts is Equal to the Whole

To paraphrase Le Corbusier, the renowned French architect and philosopher of modernism and Leong's mentor, "true art" is found in the comparison of its component parts. Each individual piece should be reducible to its essential element. When all units are stacked together, a purity of form is achieved. This is the ideal for which Po Shun Leong is striving. The works presented in this book stand as monuments erected along the path of this achievement.

Joseph Cornell. *Untitled (Dovecote),* 1950–54; and *Untitled (Compartmented Dovecote),* 1950–54.

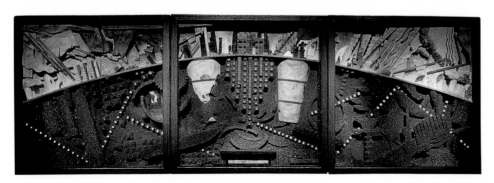

Po Shun Leong. *Triptych: The Rise and Fall of the City of Mahagonny,* 1990.

# GALLERY

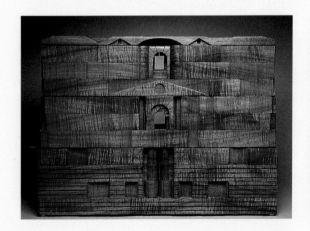

*Architecture Box*, 1987.

This is the first appearance of Po Shun's basic box form. A symmetrical, almost square shape, topped by an arching curve, houses a complex abstract interior landscape.

*Vase Shape Box*, 1988.

*Box*, 1990.

In this box and the one to the right, Po Shun continues to explore arrangements of pivoting drawers, a feature that first appears in one of his earliest designs ("Crescent Box," 1983, page 8).

*The title, dimensions, and creation date of each piece are given in the list of illustrations on page 126.*

*Tower Box*, 1988.

*Cityscape,* 1993.

This box shows extensive use of geometric and architectural elements, as well as details with a cross-hatched surface pattern, produced on the bandsaw.

The two boxes on these pages show the artist's increasing interest in visual drama, as well as his first large-scale use of pink ivory wood. The basic elements of square and tower are still evident, as is the symmetry, but the compositions are enlivened and made more complex by interior voids and irregular outlines. Each of the intricate landscapes appears like the stage of a theater.

*Twin Towers, 1991.*

*Secret Places, 1989.*

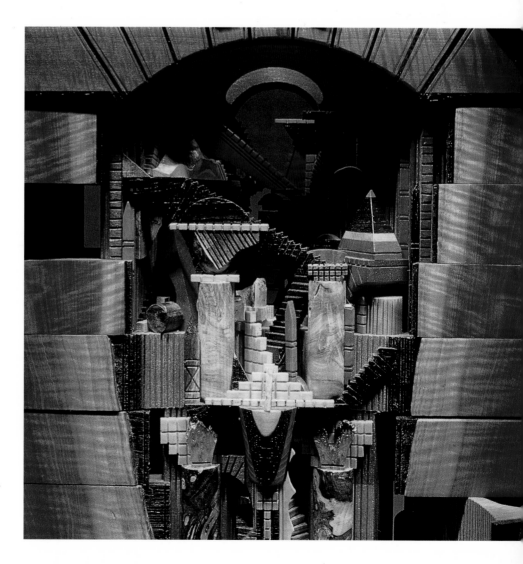

*Secret Places, 1989.* Detail.

*Tall Box,* 1992.

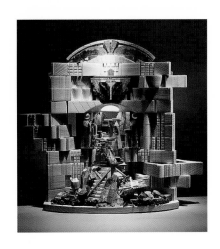

*Rise and Fall,* 1992.

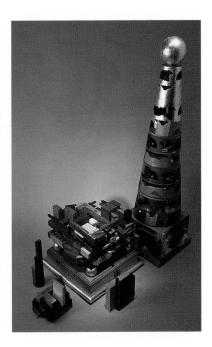

*Towers,* 1991.

*Black Landscape Box,* 1991.

*Puzzle,* 1991.

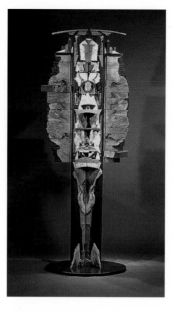

Here the artist has enlarged the box into a freestanding version. Each is exactly six feet tall.

*Tall Box,* 1989.          *Tall Box,* 1989.

Opposite: *Tall Box,* 1989. Detail.
Below: *Tall Box,* 1989. Sketches.

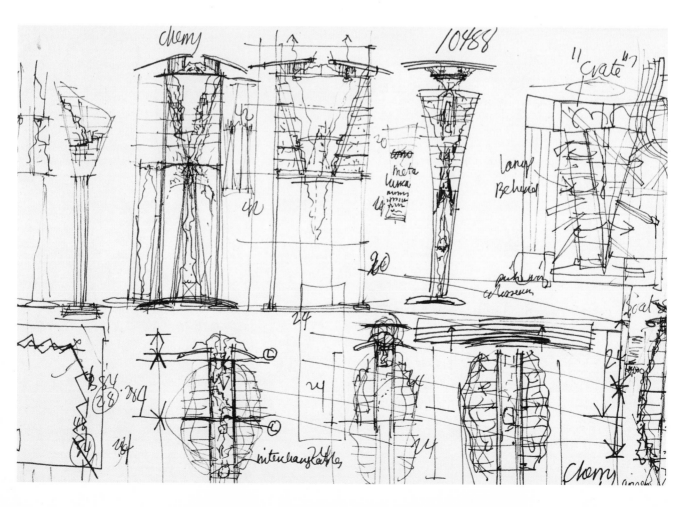

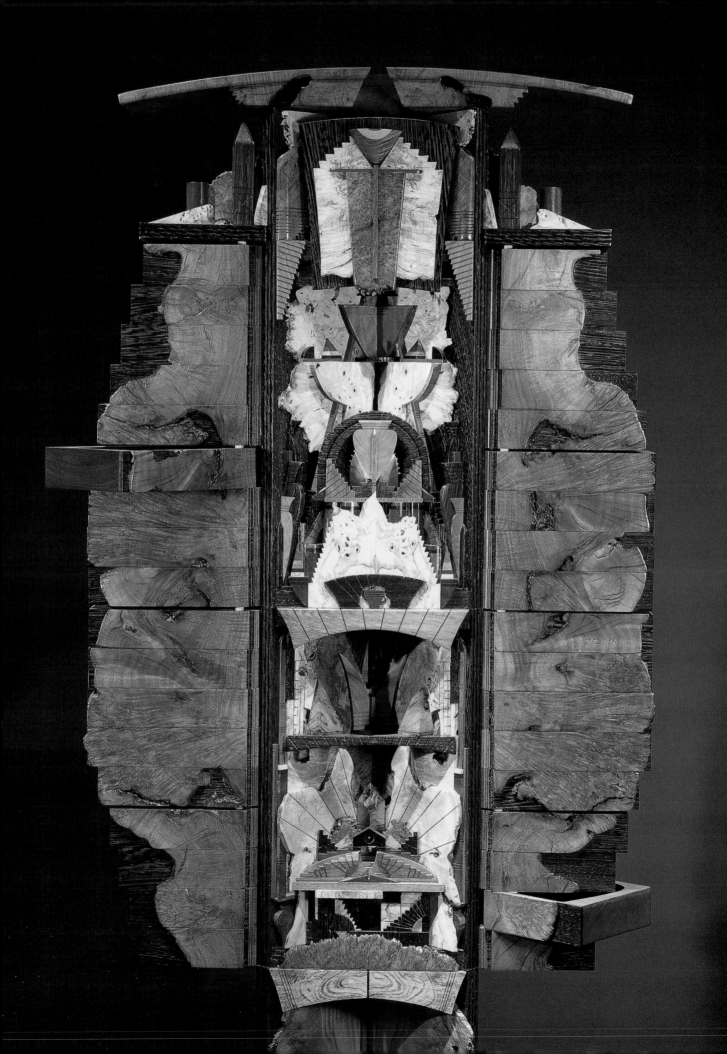

Figure, 1993.

"Poh Suan and I went to see an exhibition of sculptures by the German artist Max Ernst. I was familiar with Ernst's surrealist paintings of the 1920s and '30s, but these sculptures were nothing like that—they were quite playful. With them as inspiration, I decided to try a box that might capture the playfulness, while also using the human figure. The faces in this piece are movable, so that you can change their expression."

*Totem,* 1997, right; Detail below.

The tower form, cross-hatched drawer front, square-within-circle motif, and series of repeating shapes are visual themes that recur in Po Shun's box designs.

*Pylon*, 1996.

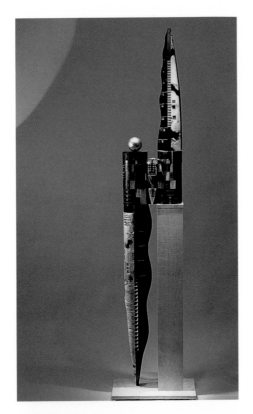

*Up/Down,*
1993.

*Tall Box,* 1994.

*Sculptural
Box,* 1996.

*Totem Boxes,*
1997.

In the designs on these two pages the artist continues to explore the tower form, and introduces the oval as a framing shape.

*Figurative Box*, 1996.

The muted palette of "In Construction," 1995 (opposite), and "Figurative Box," 1996 (below) is created by bleaching and dyeing wenge, normally a black wood. The colors of these two pieces represent a striking departure from the warm, natural wood tones of most of Po Shun's work, just as the irregular shapes contrast with his customary symmetry.

*Box on Box,* 1994.

*White on Black,* 1994.

Opposite: *Modern Times,* 1994.

"Modern Times" is the first of a series of wall-mounted boxes. Its title was suggested by the 1936 Charlie Chaplin film of the same name.

*Pendulum Box,* 1994.

Po Shun deliberately designs his work to invite the viewer to interact with it by touching. In "Pendulum Box," the boats on top sway back and forth as the ebony and pink ivorywood pendulums are moved.

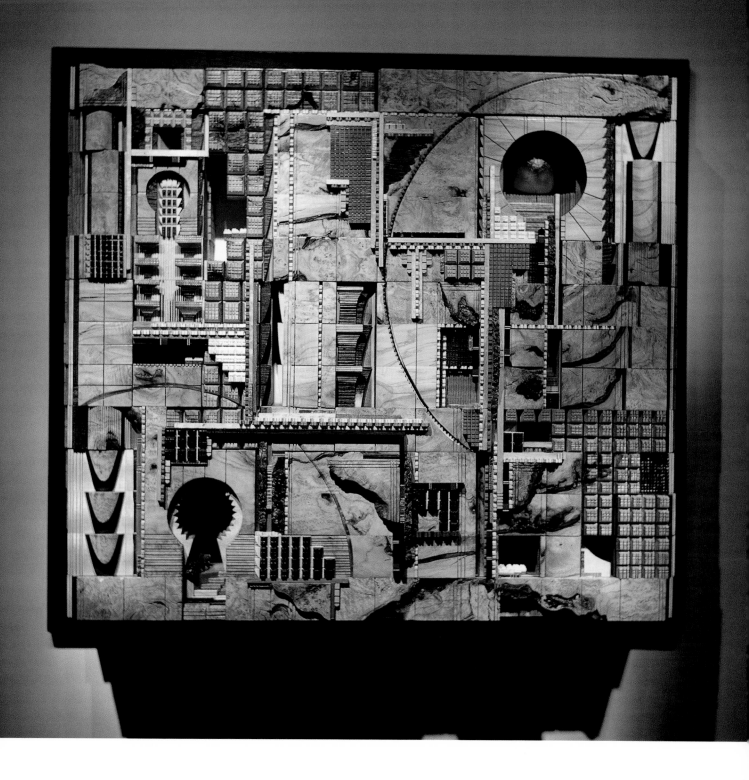

*Cosmos Box*, 1994.

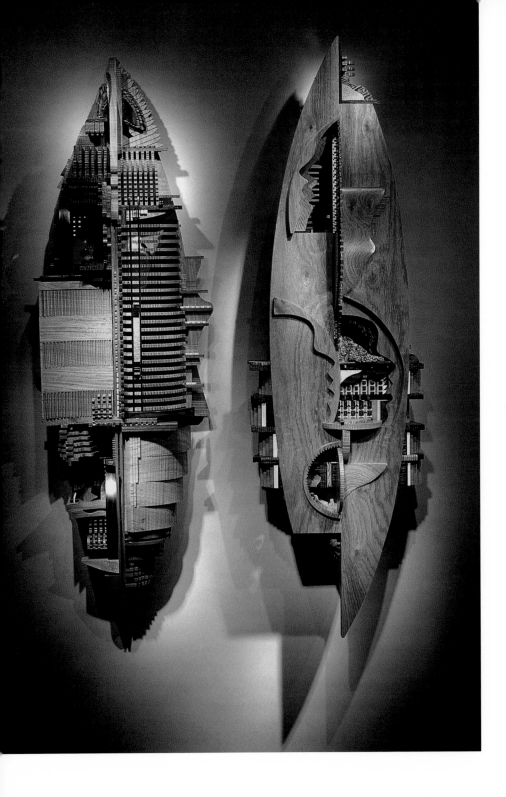

*Mask Boxes,* 1994. From a series of twelve.

These were inspired by a visit to the Michael Rockefeller Wing at the Metropolitan Museum of Art in New York, with its superb collection of Oceanic and Asmat tribal art.

1990

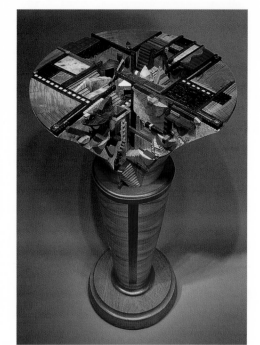

1990

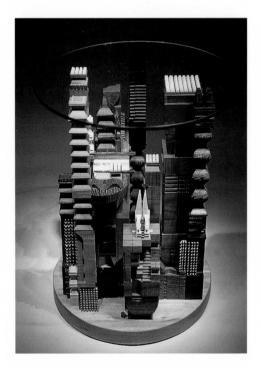

1996

1995

In addition to boxes, Po Shun has applied his visual vocabulary of form, detail, and color to furniture. These four glass-topped side tables, containing many of the motifs used in the boxes, were created in 1990 (top), 1995 (bottom right) and 1996 (bottom left).

*Side Table*, 1996. Detail.

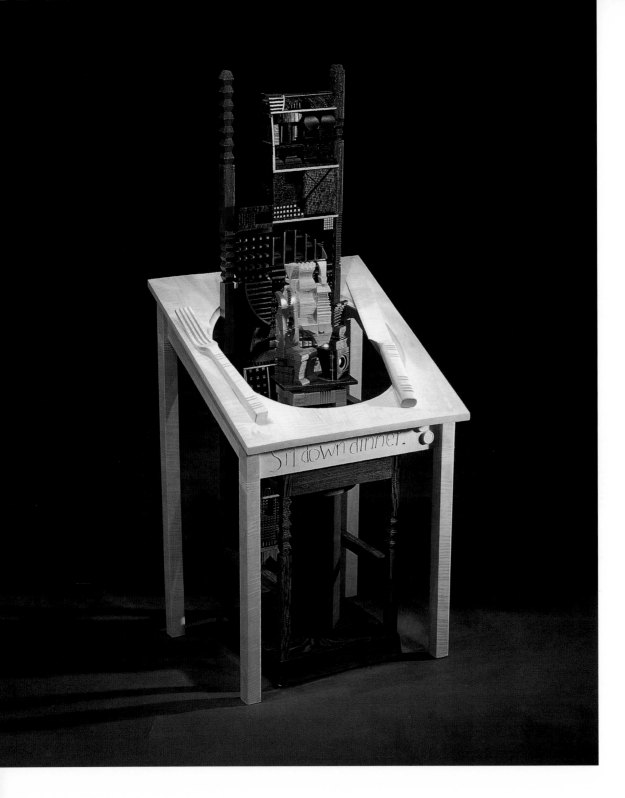

*Sit Down Dinner*, 1997.

"Sit Down Dinner" is the latest in the artist's continuing exploration of new ways to conceptualize that basic article of furniture known as the chair. This tongue-in-cheek version was shown in an exhibition entitled "Food, Glorious Food: Artists on Eating."

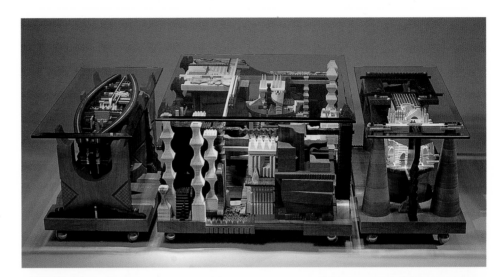

*Set of Three Coffee Tables, 1995.*

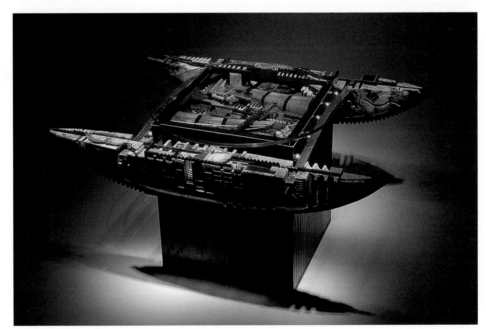

*Coffee Table, 1993.*

*Set of Two Coffee Tables,* 1996.

The inspiration for this commissioned set of tables was the contrast between destruction and rebuilding exemplified by the city of Berlin, Germany. Pieces of concrete and bolts salvaged from the Berlin Wall are incorporated in the dark table, made of black-stained ash, which represents destruction and chaos. Its damaged buildings, sculpted in buckeye burl, include the lone cathedral spire that survived the Second World War. The light table, titled "Construction in Progress," portrays the rebuilt city in bleached maple above a mahogany base.

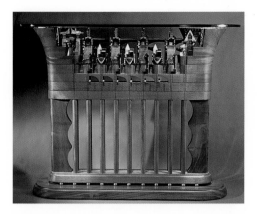

1991

1992

1993

1994

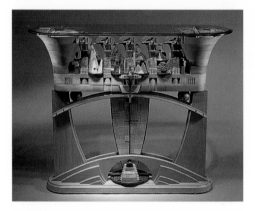

1995

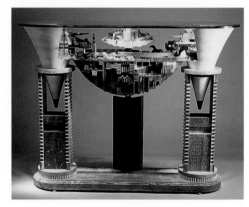

1996

1996

1997

*Console table*, 1991. Detail.

These glass-topped console tables, created between 1991 and 1997, offer eight variations on a theme.

Above: *Console table*, 1997.
Opposite: *Console table*, 1997, shown with glass top removed.

*Pompeii Vessel #1, 1989.*

*Pompeii Vessel: On Fire, 1990.*

Previous pages: *Writing Desk and Chair, 1997.*

The collector who commissioned this desk and chair asked for a piece with a monumental quality, that when closed would look like a work of art. The intricately
detailed upper doors open to reveal portions of a sculpted city, which is lighted;
the panel below them opens downward, its inner surface becoming the desktop.
Between the two banks of drawers, the white city begins, rising into a landscape of
columns, pyramids, and hills. Centered beneath the curved roof is a golden orb, traditional emblem of harmony and power.

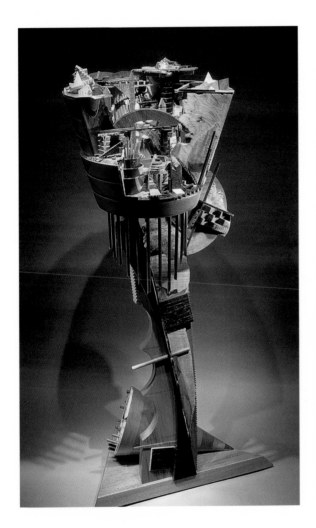

*Pompeii Vessel: Chaos*, 1991.

*Pompeii Vessel: Enclosure*, 1991.

The inspiration for this series, which includes ten freestanding pieces characterized by vase-like shapes, was the eruption of Mt. Vesuvius in Italy in 79 A.D., and the subsequent death of the town of Pompeii, buried within hours under volcanic ash.

*Ark,* 1996.

*Rocking Ark,* 1990.

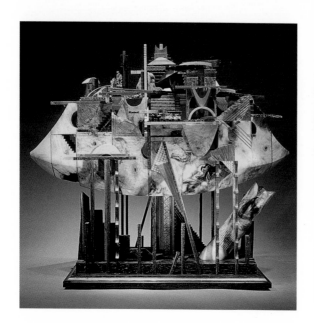

*Ark,* 1989.

*Water World,* 1996.

As a young boy, Po Shun spent many hours playing with a full-scale wooden model of an ocean liner. This ship had a substantial influence on his later work, both concretely (as a marvel of intricate complexity, and as a design built to accommodate human needs), and metaphorically (as a vessel carrying the ideas and ideals of civilization). This series of Arks includes some of Po Shun's most imaginative designs; the burl and ebony hull of "Ark," 1990 (opposite) shows his use of the natural beauty of wood at its most spectacular.

Opposite: *Ark,* 1990.

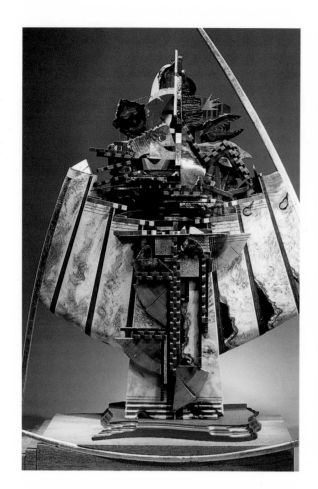 

*Warrior,* 1990; Detail, right.

"Warrior" evolved from the artist's search for a design based on the human figure. As he sketched, the Biblical notion of swords turned into plowshares—implements of destruction re-formed as tools of creation—came to mind.

Opposite: *Figure,* 1993; Details.

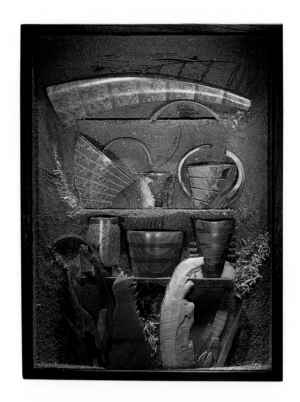

*Mind Over Matter, 1990.*                    *Kiln, 1990.*

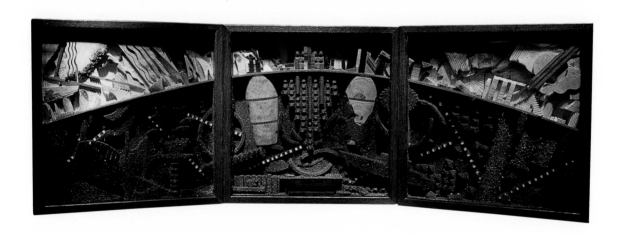

*The Rise and Fall of the City of Mahagonny, 1990.*

This series of collages, each framed behind glass in a wall-mounted box, includes constructed elements, found objects, and sawdust.

*The Rise and Fall of the City of Mahagonny*, 1990. Detail.

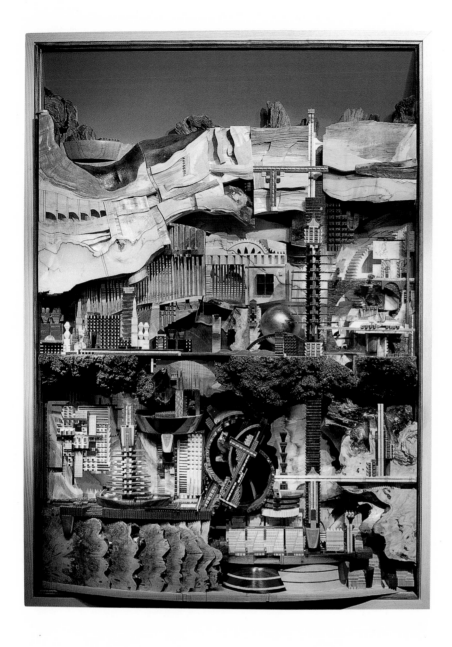

*Mesa Verde,* 1994.

Measuring 55" x 40" x 9", this complex wall-mounted collage is a commissioned work that was inspired by cliff dwellings in Mesa Verde, Colorado, abandoned over eight hundred years ago. The design integrates the ruins of these ancient habitations with the advanced urban engineering of the modern era. Tunnels, bridges, vertical transportation veins, cooling fins, a dam, power sources and factory wheels accompany the dwellings, along with carved tunnels and hidden caves. The entire city is topped by a plateau where antennae and air shafts pierce the blue sky. The sky is lit by a concealed lighting strip, whose color may be adjusted to create the warm colors of sunset.

Drawing of Mesa Verde,
Colorado, 1200 A.D.

# CREATING ART BOXES

Pencil Box

page 78

Wheel Box

page 84

Ancient Ruins Box

page 90

Ark Box

page 98

Sculptural Box

page 106

# CREATING ART BOXES

Po Shun Leong's boxes are all constructed using the same basic approach: each begins as a simple underlying structure, which is then detailed with glued-on architectural elements, geometric shapes, and natural wood accents. As the artist puts it:

*Like Chinese food, it's all in the cutting. Begin by preparing in advance a large variety of parts of all sorts and sizes, being sure to utilize every bit of the wood, including the defects, scrap, and cutouts. Then to make a finished box, you assemble the parts into interesting combinations at whim—different each time—so there's a large menu in every piece. It's useful to have a general plan for what you want to accomplish, but remember that you're creating a feast for the senses, so don't be too bound by your plan.*

To show how such a straightforward approach can produce such extraordinary results, this section presents an overview of Po Shun's creative process. We begin with a tour of famous and legendary landscapes and places throughout the world that serve as sources of inspiration, and then follow the artist in his studio, as he sketches and models new box design ideas.

Pages 68-71 give a complete listing of the boxmaking tools, machinery, and equipment used by Po Shun, along with his refreshingly minimalist views on sanding and finishing. Names of the wood species he uses follow on Page 74-5.

For boxmakers interested in hands-on exploration, Po Shun has created five box designs specifically for this book: a Pencil Box, Wheel Box, Ark Box, Ancient Ruins Box, and Sculptural Box (Pages 76-111). Each includes an exploded diagram, a dimensioned materials list, and complete step-by-step how-to instructions.

Pages 112-117 provide additional how-to instructions for making architectural details such as pyramids, obelisks, columns, and cones. Nothing goes to waste in Po Shun's studio: sawdust and shavings are transformed into colorful boxed collages (pages 118-121); scrap wood, including failed and broken projects contributed by other woodworkers, is incorporated into fresh designs (pages 122-123). Finally, pages 124-5 show how the artist recycles his own work, utilizing portions of early pieces to create new ones.

# INSPIRATION

*My boxes are like the great cities of the world. They're built up of layer upon layer of different materials, textures and shapes, each reflecting the influence of a different culture, people, or period of history.*

Po Shun Leong has travelled widely, and lived in several different countries. The unique forms of his work arise as images of real places he has experienced, like those illustrated here, which are then mingled and blended with the legendary and mythic places he sees in his mind's eye.

*For thousands of years, the landscapes and structures in these drawings have inspired poets, musicians, painters, and architects. Look at them with your creative eye open, and you'll find you retain what you see. The visual memories become indelible, and even if you didn't want them to, you couldn't keep them from surfacing in your work.*

Many of the spires and stairs, balconies and battlements, minarets and towers that enliven Po Shun's work were adapted from the originals shown here. Perhaps more important, these helped shape his awareness of grandeur and wonder, and sharpened his senses to the importance of the magnificent and the sublime.

Occasionally one of his pieces can be directly traced to a historical source, such as The Temple of Delphi. Constructed in ancient Greece early in the Fourth Century B.C., near the modern-day city of Athens, this temple was the source for the Ancient Ruins Box on pages 90-97. An image of the Chrysler Building in New York City, designed by William Van Alen and completed in 1930, (top of page 61, second from left) appears in the set of coffee tables shown on pages 40-41.

The same set includes what appears to be the ruins of a Mayan temple, next to the bombed-out spire of a church in Berlin. The complex design of this piece, commissioned by a German client, also incorporates bolts and remnants of concrete from the Berlin Wall.

Opposite page, left to right: The Ruins of Delphi, Greece, home of the most famous oracle in the ancient world; Petra's open air theater cut into the rock; Rock-cut facade of the Khasneh al Raroun also in Petra, Jordan; Dim-Moon City of Delight, Baghdad.

The skyscrapers of Chicago, New York, and Houston.

Mont-St-Michel, France; Fortress of Kronborg, Denmark, the setting for Hamlet; The bright corals and submarine caves of Nail Island, Thailand; Stone steps where pilgrims bathe in the Ganges River, Benares, India.

The castle of Neuschwanstein, Germany; The Potala, fortress palace of the Dalai Lama in Tibet; Ornate pinnacles in Rangoon; The pyramids of Giza.

The ruins of Luxor on the Nile; Bhaktapur, Nepal; Machu Picchu, Peru; The temple of the Giant Jaguar, Tikal, Guatemala.

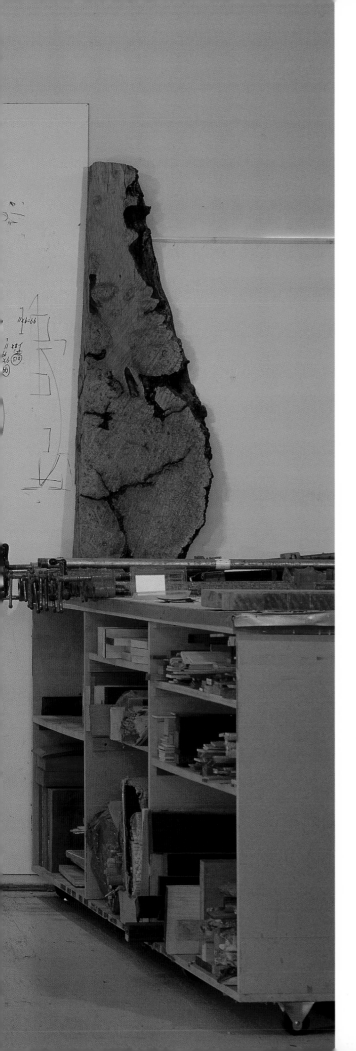

# SKETCHING

The most important wall in Po Shun's studio contains a large drawing board, on which, in two dimensions, the artist conceives and then works through the development of a new piece. He draws in felt tip marker, fluid and easy to modify, on an erasable board. Because he works life size, and standing up, his entire body gets physically involved in the act of drawing. This lets him sense, weigh, almost feel each line and form he sketches. One of the results of this approach to design is good exercise; another is that it gives Po Shun's work the sense of aliveness, of physical presence, that makes such an impact on even a casual observer.

Po Shun's working style emphasizes the importance of the spontaneous. As he develops a design idea, he is careful to remain open to any new direction that may suggest itself, based on a whim, an intuition, a mistake or an accident. He writes:

> In designing a box, it's easy to get bogged down with too much planning, too much of a preconception of where you should go. You don't really need a preconceived idea, and I often begin work without one. You just start, and let the rest be spontaneous.

The two boxes on the pedestal to the artist's right are models of a totem design similar to the one he is working at. Beyond them, the drawing board is flanked by a slab of figured cherry burl. On the wall to the artist's left is one of the first in a series of small sawdust collages.

# MODELS

Like life-size drawing, small-scale models give the artist an opportunity to explore the visual impact of a particular form, combination of materials, or set of proportions before committing to a larger, more costly, and more time-consuming final version.

Po Shun fashioned these models, the tallest of which stands 6" high, from scrap woods, held together with hot melt glue. Surrounding the models are photographs of some of the completed pieces to which they led.

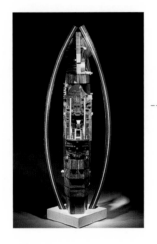

*Pylon Box,* 1996.

Right: *Pompeii Vessel,* 1991.
Far right: *Rocking Ark,* 1990.

*Console Table,* 1996. Detail.

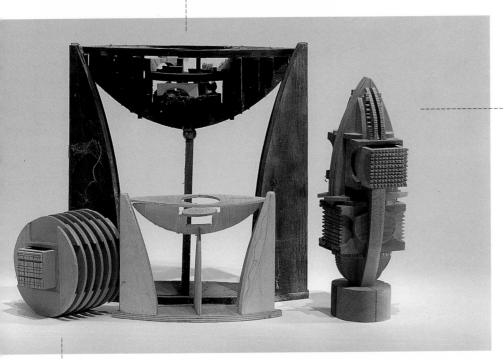

*Sculptural Box,* 1997.

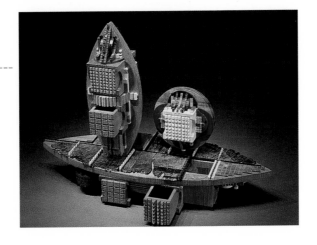

*Horizontal Box,* 1997.

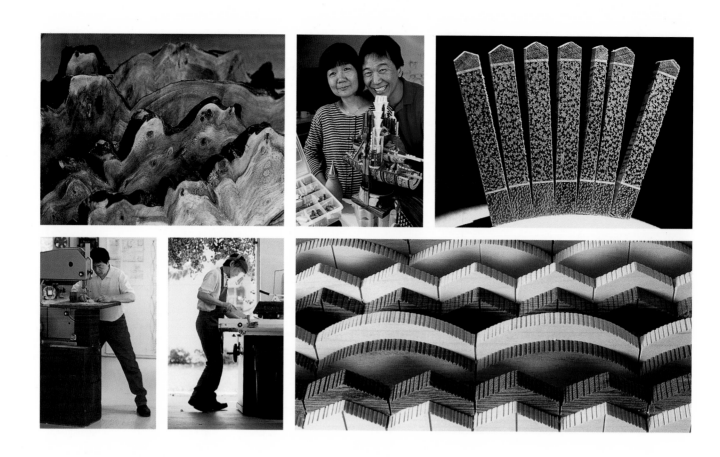

# S T U D I O

Like many woodworkers, Po Shun creates his masterpieces in a workshop no bigger than a two-car garage, augmented in good weather by a concrete apron under an overhanging roof, where the tablesaw, router table, and stationary sander are kept. His spray booth is an outdoor area that includes his side of the neighbor's back fence.

Indoors, flanking the drawing board, two tables hold work in progress, assisted as needed by a couple of wheeled carts. One end of the studio serves as the lumberyard, where surfaced boards stand in neat rows to await selection. Stacks of boards and piles of burl in varying stages of air-drying take up most of the patio and the real garage, which Po Shun's family car—like that of so many woodworkers—has never entered.

At the other end of the studio is a maze of shelves and drawers, each holding dozens of Po Shun's trademark architectural and geometric shapes. Scattered atop the drawers and hanging on the walls above them is the shop archives, a collection that includes early work, great ideas that somehow didn't pan out, and related favorite, funny, and sentimental things.

# TOOLS

Trained in the abstract manner as an architect, rather than concretely, as a wood-worker, Po Shun views tools solely as a means to an end. He has developed his wood-working techniques, and the tools to produce them, for simplicity, efficiency, safety, and ease of use.

The five how-to projects on Pages 76 through 111, as well as all the work shown in this book, were made using the following tools.

| | | |
|---|---|---|
| 1. | **Band saw** | Po Shun uses a 20-inch model with a 1/4" blade, 10 teeth per inch. In addition to cutting curved shapes, this tool produces the various cross-hatch and scoring details that are so prevalent throughout his work. |
| 2. | **Table saw** | A 10-inch tilting-arbor model is the most useful. Crosscut and rip cuts can both be made using a single blade, such as a 50-tooth ATB combination. Blades should be carbide tipped, and cleaned as needed with spray-on oven cleaner. |
| 3. | **Planer and Joiner** | These are essential for giving boards uniform thickness and flat surfaces and edges. When blades are kept sharp and free of nicks, the need for sanding can be dramatically reduced, and in many cases even eliminated. |
| 4. | **Drum sander** | Po Shun uses a pneumatic version, with a sanding drum that is inflated. This makes it possible to sand curved shapes. |
| 5. | **Stationary belt sander** | A useful size is 6" x 48", available from most tool shops and catalogs. For small parts, such as those in the five how-to projects, a hand-held 4" x 24" sander can be utilized, secured upside-down in a jig built specially for that purpose. |

| | | |
|---|---|---|
| 6. | **Router table** | A hand-held router is a standard woodshop tool. It can be made more versatile by creating a table with the tool mounted below the table surface. This makes it possible to pass a workpiece over the cutter. In the Wheel Box (pages 84–9), the ⅜" dado on the box body was made in this manner. |
| 7. | **Drill Press** | Either a freestanding or bench size model can be used to drill holes for dowels and screws, and to bore drawer cavities using a flat-bottomed bit. |
| 8. | **Air Compressor** | With attachments such as a spraygun and blowgun, this machine makes it possible to spray lacquer, blow excess flocking out of drawers, and perform a variety of cleanup operations. |
| 9. | **Dust collection system** | For both safety and ease of operation, all stationary tools should be connected to a central dust collection system. |
| 10. | **Hand tools** | As illustrated in the photograph opposite, Po Shun's shop has basic tools such as sanding pads, chisels, utility knives, hammers, a square, an electric screwgun, masking tape, bar-, spring- and C-clamps, gloves, a dust brush, drawing implements, and white and hot-melt glue. |

## 11. **Safety**

Woodworking is inherently dangerous. The raw material itself can be heavy, sharp edged and splintery, and the tools used to fabricate it are all potentially lethal. These factors, combined with noxious dust, harmful chemicals, high noise levels, and large quantities of electricity, produce an environment in which disfiguring, crippling, or even fatal injury can occur in dozens of unforeseen ways. To operate a safe woodshop, always keep this in mind.

The risk of injury can never be completely removed, but it can be reduced to an acceptable level by strict observation of certain guidelines.

1.  For safe operation of a table saw and other power tools, make sure you read, understand and adhere to manufacturer's instructions.

2.  Never allow fingers to come near any moving blade or cutter. Use a push stick.

3.  When using hand-held carving tools, keep your hands out of the path of the tool. Make sure the workpiece is securely held in place.

4.  Always wear a respirator or dust mask in the shop. Always wear eye and ear protection when using power tools.

5.  Wear appropriate clothing. A heavy work apron will protect the lap and midsection, and proper footwear will soften the impact of the occasional dropped log or chisel.

6.  Never perform any operation without being satisfied that you understand it and are comfortable with it.

7.  Keep your mind on your work. Do not allow your attention to wander, especially when performing repetitive operations.

8.  Never work when you are tired, in a hurry, or simply not in the mood to work. It is better to stop, or find something to do outside the shop for a while. Return refreshed and in the proper frame of mind.

# SANDING

*I hate sanding, and have worked hard to come up with fabrication techniques that hold it to an absolute minimum. First, by keeping the planer and joiner blades very sharp, and free of nicks, I ensure that the surface of the wood comes out smooth enough that often it requires no sanding at all.*

*Second, I avoid traditional joinery wherever possible. For example, my drawers are made from a single block, or at most a block with a pair of sides glued on. The fewer parts there are in an assembly, the fewer joints will require abrasive clean-up.*

*In most people's boxes, the drawer fronts are made to shine like little jewels. Too much sanding for me, which has given rise to the cross-hatch pattern you see on all my drawer fronts.*

*Finally, my box designs involve gluing layers of details onto a basic substructure. Most of these details are cut on the bandsaw, whose blade leaves a slight textural roughness, which I prefer. Plus, they need no sanding whatsoever.*

*I don't want to give the impression that sanding is never appropriate. On the contrary: finely polished hardwood plays an important role in my designs. A nice piece of something like cherry burl or pink ivorywood shows so beautifully when properly sanded and finished. It's just that I want the effort of sanding to go where it will be well repaid.*

# FINISHING

The five how-to projects on pages 76 through 111, as well as the work in the Gallery section, have a hand-rubbed oil finish, followed by two coats of water-based spray lacquer. Oil is applied with a brush or cloth, and the excess then wiped off following manufacturer's instructions. After the oil has thoroughly dried, the first coat of lacquer is applied with a spray gun connected to an air compressor. (For boxmakers whose studios lack this equipment, water-based lacquer is also available in individual spray cans). The second coat of lacquer is sprayed on following light sanding.

# BLEACH

Particularly for projects such as the Pencil Box (pages 76–83), which incorporate the black hardwood called wenge, Po Shun often bleaches the wood prior to finishing. This heightens the contrast between light and dark fibers. After assembling the pencil box, apply bleach, wearing protective clothing, impermeable gloves and eye protection, and following manufacturer's instructions. Apply oil and lacquer only after the bleach is thoroughly dry.

# WOODS USED

The factors that go into the selection of woods include availability, workability, contrast, color, figure, and grain. When purchasing lumber, be sure that it comes from a certified source that practices sustainable yield forest management.

Lacewood

Narra

Zebrawood

Cherry Burl

Gold Leaf

Koa

Pau Amarillo

Pink Ivory

Purpleheart

Birds-eye Maple

Tulipwood

Maple

Black Acacia

Cherry

Silk Oak

Mahogany

Palm Wood

Buckeye Burl

Bocote

Macassar Ebony

This sculptural pencil box, whose towers evoke the soaring skyscrapers of New York City, makes a beautiful addition to any desk. The light and dark woods are maple and wenge, which have been bleached following the procedure on page 73. The number, size and placement of the columns, towers, and other details are variable, and may be changed at the will of the boxmaker.

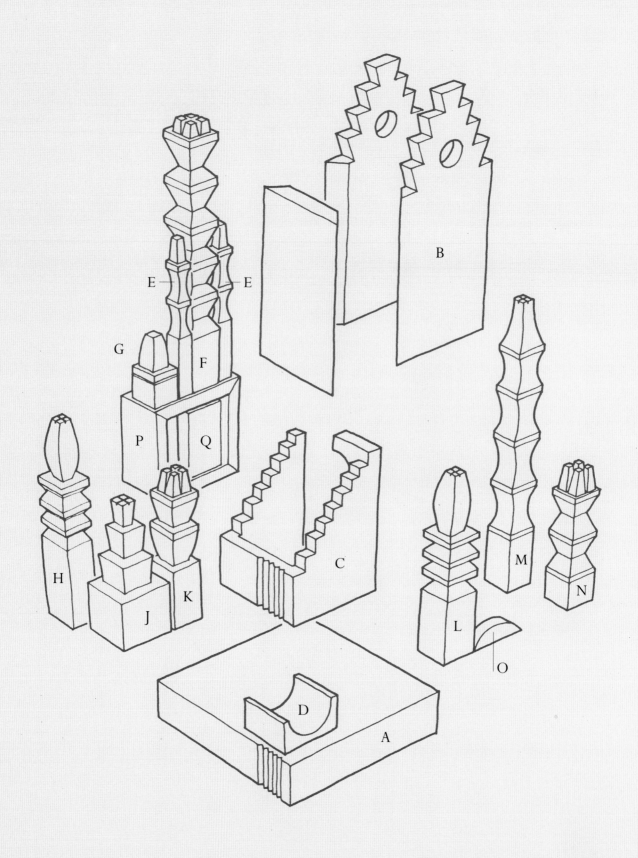

# PENCIL BOX

| Part | Description | Dimensions | Quantity |
|------|-------------|------------|----------|
| A | Base | ¾" x 5" x 5" | 1 |
| B | Pencil holder side | ⅜" x 2⅝" x 6½" | 4 |
| C | Paper clip holder side | ⅜" x 2⅝" x 3½" | 4 |
| D | Paper clip dish | 1⅛" x 1¹³⁄₁₆" x 1¹³⁄₁₆" | 4 |
| E | Detail, tower | ⁷⁄₁₆" x ⁷⁄₁₆" x 4" | 2 |
| F | Detail, tower | ¹³⁄₁₆" x ¹³⁄₁₆" x 6⅜" | 1 |
| G | Detail, tower | ¹³⁄₁₆" x ¹³⁄₁₆" x 1⅝" | 1 |
| H | Detail, tower | ¾" x ¾" x 4½" | 1 |
| J | Detail, tower | 1⅜" x 1⅜" x 3⅝" | 1 |
| K | Detail, tower | ¾" x ¾" x 4" | 1 |
| L | Detail, tower | ¾" x ¾" x 4½" | 1 |
| M | Detail, tower | ¾" x ¾" x 7¼" | 1 |
| N | Detail, tower | ¾" x ¾" x 3⅜" | 1 |
| O | Detail, half-moon | ⅜" x 1¼" diameter | 1 |
| P | Detail, window | ⅜" x 1" x 2⅝" | 1 |
| Q | Detail, half cylinder | ⅞" x 1⁹⁄₁₆" x 1¹³⁄₁₆" | 1 |

- Mill the base on the tablesaw.

- Make Part B, the pencil holder, and Part C, the paper clip holder, as a single square tube by milling four pieces of wood ⅛" thick, 2⅝" wide, and 12 inches long. This tube will later be crosscut to produce Part B and Part C, as well as Part P. Use a dark wood such as walnut or wenge (the wood shown in the photographs); the contasting light colored elements of the project are made from maple. ▶

- Set the tablesaw at a 45 degree angle and rip a miter on the long edges of each of the four sides. Sand the inside faces.

- Lay the four sides flat on the workbench, with long edges touching and miters facing down. Use masking tape to tape the parts together. ▶

- Turn the entire taped assembly over and place a bead of glue in the trough formed by each pair of miters. Apply glue to the faces of the final two miters, and fold the assembly into a square tube. Use more tape to hold the final seam. Test the assembly for square. ▶

- If glue has squeezed through to the inside surfaces of the tube, wait an hour or so until the glue has set, then carefully remove any excess with a sharp chisel.

- Use the table saw to crosscut the square tube to the appropriate dimensions for the pencil holder, paper clip holder, and the window, Part P. ▶

- Wrap masking tape around the outside of the two largest tubes. With a pencil and straight edge, draw the stepped pattern for Part B and Part C. ▶

- Use the drill press to drill the decorative hole in the pencil holder. To prevent tear-out when the drill bit penetrates the inner surface of the side, place a scrap block of wood inside the tube before drilling. ▼

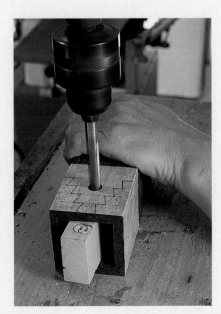

- Bandsaw the shapes of Part B and Part C. ▼

- Mill blanks for the towers (Parts E through N) on the table saw, and draw their outlines in pencil. Bandsaw the towers. ▼

- Mill Part D, the paper clip dish, from a 1¹³⁄₁₆" cube of the dark wood. The resulting half-cylinder becomes Part Q.

- Assemble and glue the parts on the base. ▼

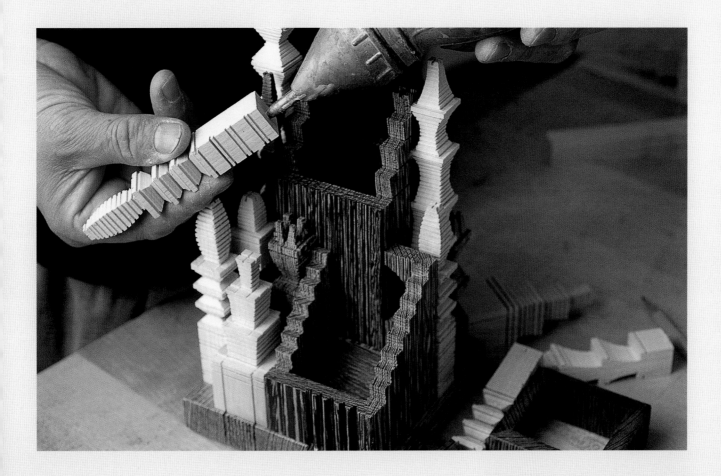

- Following the instructions on page 73, use spray bleach to lighten the wenge parts of the pencil holder. Then apply an oil finish, followed by spray lacquer. ▶

# WHEEL BOX

*The oldest known wooden disk, a Sumerian chariot wheel dated to 3500 B.C., was the inspiration for this simple yet strikingly original design, in which a book-matched wheel of figured walnut is pierced by a mahogany box that holds a maple drawer. The woods used, as well as the diameter of the wheel and dimensions of the box, may be modified to create an endless variety of combinations.*

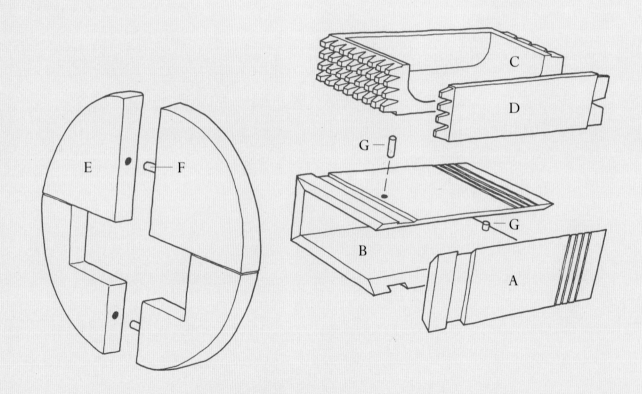

# WHEEL BOX

| Part | Description | Dimensions | Quantity |
|------|-------------|------------|----------|
| A | Box side | $\frac{5}{16}$" x $2\frac{1}{2}$" x 10" | 2 |
| B | Box top/bottom | $\frac{5}{16}$" x $4\frac{3}{4}$" x 10" | 2 |
| C | Drawer body | $1\frac{3}{4}$" x $3\frac{1}{2}$" x $9\frac{3}{4}$" | 1 |
| D | Drawer side | $\frac{1}{4}$" x $1\frac{1}{4}$" x $9\frac{3}{4}$" | 2 |
| E | Half wheel | $\frac{5}{8}$" x $4\frac{1}{2}$" x 9" | 2 |
| F | Wheel connecting dowel | $\frac{3}{8}$" x $\frac{3}{4}$" | 2 |
| G | Drawer stop dowel | $\frac{1}{4}$" x $\frac{1}{2}$" | 2 |

- Mill Parts A and B, the box top, bottom, and sides, from sustainable yield mahogany or any comparable neutral-toned wood. Sand the inside and outside faces of the parts.

- Set the tablesaw at a 45 degree angle and rip a miter on the long edges of each of the four sides.

- Lay the four sides flat on the workbench, with long edges touching and miters facing down. Use masking tape to tape the parts together.

- Turn the entire taped assembly over and place a bead of glue in the trough formed by each pair of miters. (This technique is shown in the previous project, on page 80). Apply glue to the faces of the final two miters, and fold the assembly into a square tube. Use more tape to hold the final seam. Test the assembly for square.

- If glue has squeezed through to the inside surfaces of the tube, wait an hour or so until the glue has set, then carefully remove any excess with a sharp chisel.

- Using a router or a tablesaw with a dado blade, mill a ⅝" wide dado ¼" deep around the box body, ½" in from one end. The wheel will set in this dado. ◀

- Just behind the dado, drill a ¼" diameter hole for Part G, the drawer-stop dowel, which prevents the drawer from coming out the front of the box. Drill a similar hole on the underside of the box, ½" in from the back edge. This will prevent the drawer from coming out the back. ◀

- On the table saw, mill a single block of maple or other light colored wood for the drawer body. Bandsaw out the inner cavity. Mill the drawer sides from the same wood, glue them to the drawer body, and clamp until the glue is dry. Trim any excess material off the front and back of the drawer with the tablesaw. ▼

- With a pencil and straight edge, mark the cross-hatch detailing on the drawer front. Use the band saw to cut out the detailing. ▶

- If desired, flock the drawer interior using rayon powder flocking. With a small paintbrush, paint the interior surfaces of the drawer with latex paint the same color as the flocking material. Place the drawer and a quantity of flocking in a closed plastic container. Shake the container to distribute flocking evenly over the painted surface. When the paint is dry, clean up the top of the drawer by sanding it on the stationary belt sander, then gently blow out the excess.

- Install the rear drawer-stop dowel in the underside of the box body, and insert the drawer. Install the top drawer-stop dowel. The drawer is now fixed in place in the box, and cannot be removed.

- The wheel looks best when its two halves are bookmatched. This requires slicing a single block of wood in half, and opening the two halves like the facing pages of a book. Select a 4½" x 9" block of dark, figured wood 1½" thick. Use the bandsaw or tablesaw to rip to approximately ¾" thickness. Sand smooth. ◀

- Lay the two half wheels, Part E, on the workbench in bookmatch order and use a compass to draw a circle. With a straight edge, draw the cutouts for the box body. Bandsaw the cutouts and the arc of the circle. (Note: the two half wheels may be taped together, and the circumference and box body cutouts made in both parts at the same time.) ▶

- Sand the circumferences of the half wheels. (If the two are taped together, this may also be done at the same time). Mark the locations of Part F, the two connecting dowels, and drill for them on the drill press. Install the dowels. ▶

- Apply an oil finish, followed when dry by two coats of spray lacquer, to the two half wheels and the box. Finally, assemble the two half wheels in the slots on the box body and squeeze them together, guided by the attachment dowels.

# ANCIENT RUINS BOX

This fascinating box is based on the ruins of the ancient Greek Temple of the Oracle at Delphi. The drawer and box body are made from maple and sustainable-yield mahogany; the floor and columns are burl, and the cubes, pyramids, column sections, and other elements that lie atop the structure include maple, burl, and walnut. Each time he makes a version of this box, Po Shun changes the arrangement of these elements, and he encourages box-makers to do likewise.

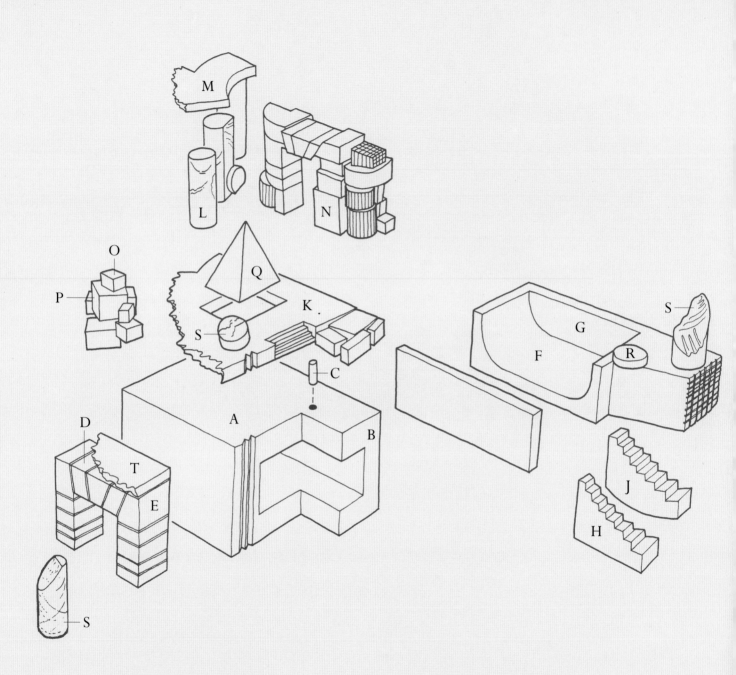

# ANCIENT RUINS BOX

| Part | Description | Dimensions | Quantity |
|---|---|---|---|
| A | Top/bottom | $\frac{3}{4}$" x 5" x 6$\frac{1}{2}$" | 2 |
| B | Side | $\frac{3}{4}$" x 3$\frac{1}{4}$" x 6$\frac{1}{2}$" | 2 |
| C | Drawer stop dowel | $\frac{1}{4}$" x 1" | 1 |
| D | Archway top | $\frac{3}{4}$" x 1$\frac{5}{8}$" x 3$\frac{1}{4}$" | 1 |
| E | Archway side | $\frac{3}{4}$" x 1$\frac{5}{8}$" x 2$\frac{13}{16}$" | 2 |
| F | Drawer body | 1$\frac{11}{16}$" x 3" x 7$\frac{1}{2}$" | 1 |
| G | Drawer side | $\frac{1}{4}$" x 1$\frac{11}{16}$" x 7$\frac{1}{2}$" | 2 |
| H | Lower stairs | 1" x 1$\frac{3}{8}$" x 1$\frac{7}{8}$" | 1 |
| J | Upper stairs | 1" x 1$\frac{3}{8}$" x 1$\frac{7}{8}$" | 1 |
| K | Floor | $\frac{3}{8}$" x 5$\frac{1}{2}$" x 6$\frac{3}{4}$" | 1 |
| L | Column | 1" diameter x 3" | 3 |
| M | Frieze | $\frac{3}{8}$" x 2$\frac{1}{2}$" x 5$\frac{1}{2}$" | 1 |
| N | Wall (assembled from 18 blocks) | 1$\frac{1}{2}$" x 3" x 4" | 1 |
| O | Detail, small block | $\frac{3}{8}$" x $\frac{1}{2}$" x $\frac{5}{8}$" | as required |
| P | Detail, large block | $\frac{7}{8}$" x $\frac{7}{8}$" x $\frac{7}{8}$" | as required |
| Q | Detail, pyramid | 1$\frac{1}{4}$" x 1$\frac{13}{16}$" x 2" | as required |
| R | Detail, circle | $\frac{3}{8}$" x 1" diameter | as required |
| S | Detail, column section | $\frac{15}{16}$" x 1" diameter | as required |
| T | Detail, burl slab | as required | as required |

- Mill the top, bottom, and sides of the box from ¼" thick sustainable-yield mahogany or similar medium-toned wood. Sand the inside and outside faces of the parts.

- Set the tablesaw at a 45 degree angle and rip a miter on the long edges of each of the four sides.

- Lay the four sides flat on the workbench, with long edges touching and miters facing down. Use masking tape to tape the parts together.

- Turn the entire taped assembly over and place a bead of glue in the trough formed by each pair of miters. (This technique is shown on page 80). Apply glue to the faces of the final two miters, and fold the assembly into a square tube. Use more tape to hold the final seam. Test the assembly for square.

- If glue has squeezed through to the inside surfaces of the tube, wait an hour or so until the glue has set, then carefully remove any excess with a sharp chisel.

- Part D/E, the archway, is a 1⅝" wide cutout bandsawed from the left front corner of the box. After cutting, score the arch on the bandsaw, then stand it upright, and glue it to the side of the box.

- For the drawer, mill a single 1¹¹⁄₁₆" thick block of solid maple on the tablesaw. Turn it on edge and bandsaw the drawer cavity. Note that since the drawer extends 2" past the front edge of the box, the cavity is only 4¼" long.

- Mill Part G, the drawer sides, on the tablesaw. Glue them to the drawer body, and clamp until the glue is dry. Trim any excess material off the front and back of the drawer with the tablesaw.

- To make Parts H and J, the stairs, bandsaw a 2" x 2" block from the front corner of the drawer. Use a pencil and straight edge to mark the outline of two staircases, and bandsaw. ▼

- Mark out the crosshatch detail on the remaining portion of the drawer front, and mill on the bandsaw. Glue the steps back in place.

- Flock the drawer interior using rayon powder flocking. With a small paintbrush, paint the interior surfaces of the drawer with latex paint the same color as the flocking material. Place the drawer and a quantity of flocking in a closed plastic container. Shake the container to distribute flocking evenly over the painted surface. When the paint is dry, clean up the top of the drawer by sanding it on the stationary belt sander, then gently blow out the excess flocking.

- Drill a ¼" diameter hole in the upper surface of the box for Part C, the drawer stop dowel. Insert the drawer, and install the dowel. The drawer can no longer be removed from the box. ▶

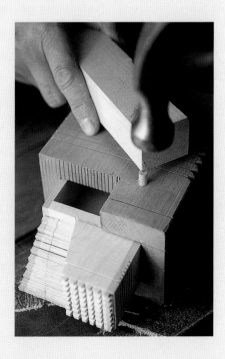

- Use the cutout from the drawer cavity to make the wall, Part N. Think of a stone wall whose blocks, although irregular, are so well fitted they require no mortar. Use a pencil to mark out three courses of blocks, and mill them on the bandsaw. Mark each block to keep track of its place for reassembly. The exterior faces of some of the blocks may be sanded, scored or otherwise detailed. The edges of some may be given a slight bevel. Reassemble the wall. ▼

- Mill Part K, the floor, from a ⅛" thick piece of burlwood, with the natural edge showing as an arc. Mill Part M, the frieze, from a similar piece of burl. The natural edges of both parts may be highlighted with gold paint.

- Mill Part L, the columns, on the bandsaw from a 3" thick chunk of burl or other figured wood. ▶

- Glue Part K, the floor, to the top of the box. Glue on Part L, Part M, and Part N, the columns, frieze, and wall. ▼

- Now that the box, drawer, and column structure are complete, the design and construction of the rest of the "ruins" are left to the imagination of the boxmaker. Use assorted column sections, burl bits, blocks, pyramids, circles, and other visually interesting elements to convey the sense of an ancient grandeur suddenly abandoned, then slowly overwhelmed by long decay.

- Apply an oil finish, and follow when dry with two coats of spray lacquer.

# ARK BOX

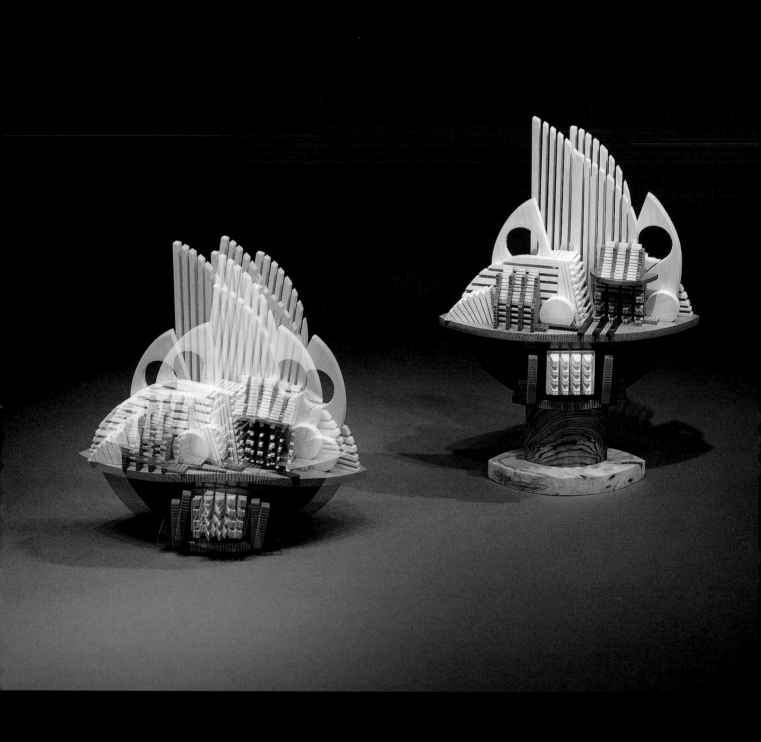

Inspired by the artist's early fascination with ship models, this project rests atop a pedestal, held in place by a dowel. The ark may be removed from the pedestal and set on a flat surface, where it will rock back and forth on its curved wenge keel. The pedestal is maple and bocote; the sustainable-yield mahogany deck holds the maple superstructure and sails.

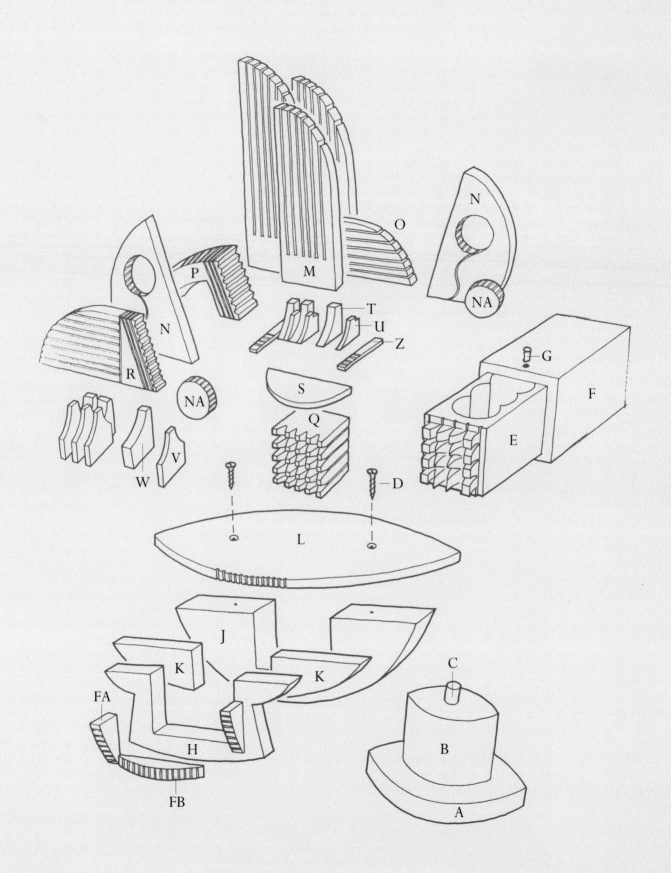

| Part | Description | Dimensions | Quantity |
|------|-------------|------------|----------|
| A | Base | $\frac{13}{16}$" x $3\frac{1}{2}$" x $6\frac{1}{4}$" | 1 |
| B | Pedestal | $1\frac{5}{8}$" x $2\frac{5}{8}$" x $3\frac{3}{8}$" | 1 |
| C | Attachment dowel | $\frac{3}{8}$" x 1" | 1 |
| D | Attachment screw | #6 x 1" | 3 |
| E | Drawer | $1\frac{13}{16}$" x $1\frac{13}{16}$" x 5" | 1 |
| F | Drawer housing side | $\frac{3}{8}$" x $2\frac{1}{2}$" x 4" | 4 |
| FA | Drawer housing frame | $\frac{3}{8}$" x $\frac{7}{8}$" x $2\frac{1}{8}$" | 4 |
| FB | Drawer housing frame | $\frac{3}{8}$" x $\frac{1}{2}$" x $2\frac{1}{2}$" | 2 |
| G | Drawer stop dowel | $\frac{1}{4}$" x $\frac{3}{4}$" | 1 |
| H | Rocker | $\frac{3}{8}$" x $3\frac{1}{4}$" x 6" | 2 |
| J | Keel | $\frac{13}{16}$" x $3\frac{1}{4}$" x $8\frac{1}{2}$" | 1 |
| K | Spacer | $\frac{3}{8}$" x $1\frac{3}{8}$" x $2\frac{1}{2}$" | 4 |
| L | Floor | $\frac{3}{8}$" x 4" x 10" | 1 |
| M | Vertical sail | $\frac{3}{8}$" x $2\frac{3}{8}$" x $6\frac{1}{4}$", $6\frac{7}{8}$", $7\frac{3}{8}$" | 3 |
| N | Circle sail | $\frac{3}{8}$" x $2\frac{1}{2}$" x 5" | 2 |
| NA | Detail, circle | $\frac{3}{8}$" x $1\frac{1}{4}$" diameter | 2 |
| O | Detail, horizontal sail | $\frac{3}{8}$" x $2\frac{1}{2}$" x $5\frac{1}{8}$" and $5\frac{3}{4}$" | 2 |
| P | Detail, stepped bridge | $\frac{13}{16}$" x 3" x 4" | 1 |
| Q | Detail, laminate block | $\frac{3}{4}$" x $1\frac{11}{16}$" x $1\frac{13}{16}$" | 1 |
| R | Detail, stepped wedge | $\frac{13}{16}$" x $1\frac{3}{8}$" x $2\frac{1}{8}$" | 1 |
| S | Detail, half circle | $\frac{1}{8}$" x $2\frac{1}{2}$" diameter | 1 |
| T | Detail, small assembly part | $\frac{1}{8}$" x 1" x 1" | 4 |
| U | Detail, small assembly part | $\frac{5}{16}$" x 1" x $1\frac{1}{4}$" | 3 |
| V | Detail, large assembly part | $\frac{1}{8}$" x $1\frac{1}{4}$" x 2" | 4 |
| W | Detail, large assembly part | $\frac{5}{16}$" x $\frac{3}{4}$" x $2\frac{1}{8}$" | 3 |
| X | Detail, scored block (not drawn) | $\frac{1}{8}$" x $\frac{3}{8}$" x $\frac{3}{8}$" | 1 |
| Y | Detail, scored block (not drawn) | $\frac{1}{8}$" x $\frac{1}{2}$" x $\frac{1}{2}$" | 3 |
| Z | Detail, scored rail | $\frac{1}{8}$" x $\frac{1}{4}$" x $1\frac{5}{8}$" | 4 |

- Mill Part A and Part B, the base and pedestal, from contrasting figured hardwoods. Sand both parts, and drill a hole for Part C, the
  attachment dowel.

- Mill Part F, the drawer housing, from walnut or a similar dark wood.
  Sand the inside and outside faces of the parts.

- Set the tablesaw at a 45 degree angle and rip a miter on the long edges
  of each of the four sides.

- Lay the four sides flat on the workbench, with long edges touching and
  miters facing down. Use masking tape to tape the parts together.

- Turn the entire taped assembly over and place a bead of glue in the
  trough formed by each pair of miters. (This technique is shown on page
  80). Apply glue to the faces of the final two miters, and fold the assembly into a square tube. Use more tape to hold the final seam. Test the
  assembly for square.

- If glue has squeezed through to the inside surfaces of the tube, wait an
  hour or so until the glue has set, then carefully remove any excess with
  a sharp chisel.

- Bandsaw the square tube to its final dimension, giving the open ends a
  curved profile (the shape is shown on the opposite page). Drill for Part
  G, the drawer stop dowel.

- Mill the drawer, Part E, from a single block of maple or similar light
  colored wood. To eliminate the need for bandsawing a drawer cavity
  and then gluing on sides, this drawer is hollowed out using three overlapping borings made with a flat-bottom bit mounted on the drill press. ▶

- Use a pencil and straight edge to mark out the drawer front crosshatch detailing. Mill on the bandsaw. ▶

- Flock the drawer interior using rayon powder flocking. With a small paintbrush, paint the interior surfaces of the drawer with latex paint the same color as the flocking material. Place the drawer and a quantity of flocking in a closed plastic container. Shake the container to distribute flocking evenly over the painted surface. When the paint is dry, clean up the top of the drawer by sanding it on the stationary belt sander, then gently blow out the excess flocking.

- Insert the drawer, and install the drawer stop dowel. The drawer can no longer be removed from its housing. ▶

- Mill Part L, the floor. Drill and countersink holes for two attachment screws. On a dark wood such as walnut or wenge, use a compass to mark out and bandsaw Parts H, J, and K, the rocker, keel, and spacers. On the underside of the keel, drill a hole for Part C, the attachment dowel. Sand curved edges as needed. ▼

- Glue together the rocker/keel/spacer assembly, setting it atop the floor as a template (but be careful not to glue it to the floor). When the assembly is dry, attach it to the underside of the floor with two attachment screws. ▲

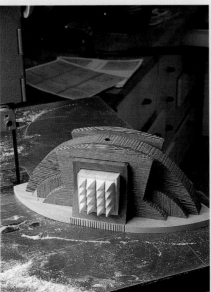

- Now that the structure underpinning the Ark is complete, the rest of the project may be designed following the imagination of the maker. In the version shown, a variety of details suggest oceangoing features such as sails, wind, movement, and cargo. Parts M, N, and O, the distinctive sails, are made by bandsawing rectangular ⅜" thick maple boards into a curved shape, and then slotting them on the tablesaw. Hand sanding is required to remove a small amount of furriness between slots. ▶

- Make Part Q, the laminate block, from four 1⁄16" thick laminates of contrasting woods. (Because of the difficulty of ripping short lengths, make a 12" long laminate, then crosscut to produce the part.) Mark out the crosshatch detailing in pencil, then mill on the bandsaw. ▲

- Use the circle cut out from Part N, the circle sail, to make Detail Part NA. Bandsaw Detail Parts P and R from blocks of maple. ▲

- From contrasting woods, bandsaw Detail Parts T and U, and Parts V and W. Each pair forms a repeating assembly. ◀

- Mill Part X, Y, and Z on the bandsaw (Part X and Y are not shown in the drawing). All are ⅛" thick blocks of various dimensions with a tic-tac-toe pattern of shallow bandsaw scoring.

- Assemble the upper portion of the Ark. ▼

- Apply an oil finish, followed when dry by two coats of spray lacquer.

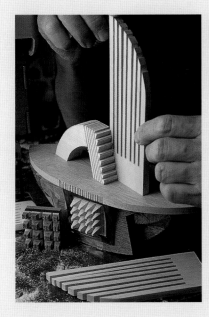
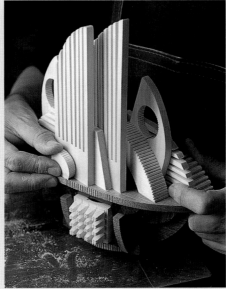

SCULPTURAL BOX

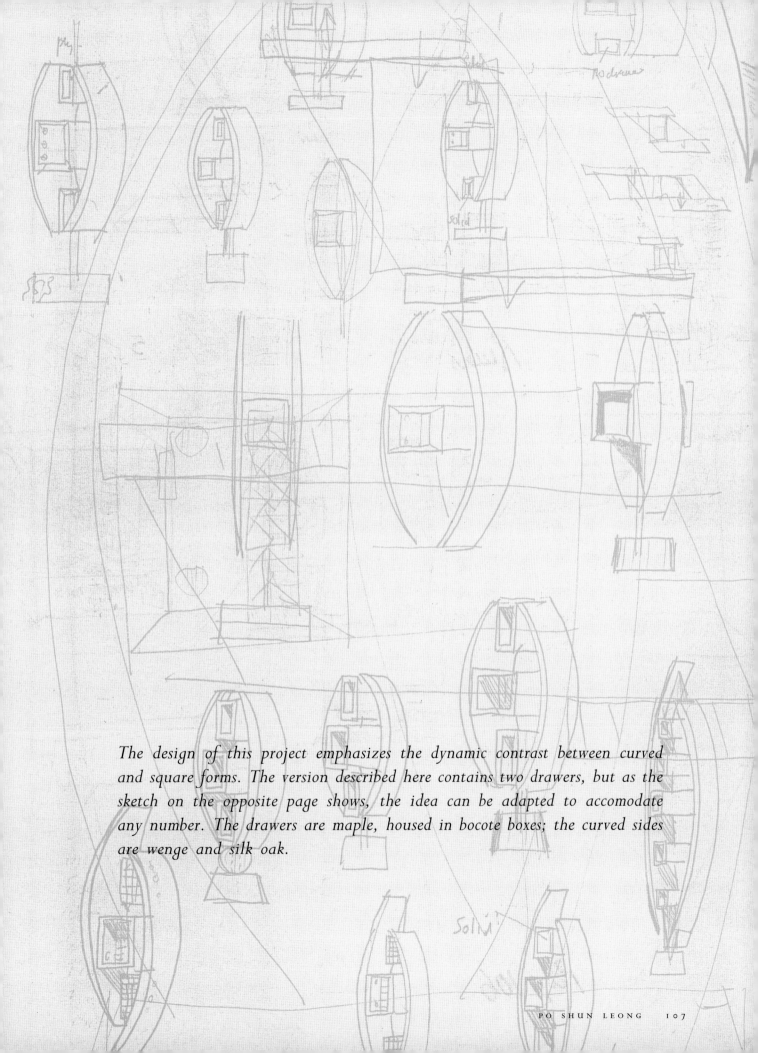

The design of this project emphasizes the dynamic contrast between curved and square forms. The version described here contains two drawers, but as the sketch on the opposite page shows, the idea can be adapted to accomodate any number. The drawers are maple, housed in bocote boxes; the curved sides are wenge and silk oak.

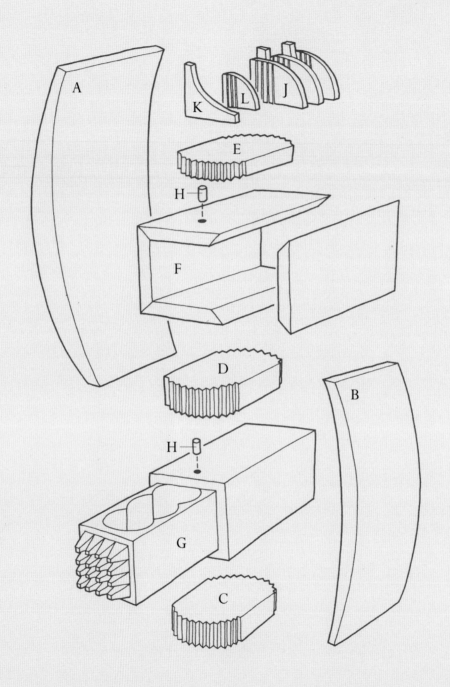

# SCULPTURAL BOX

| Part | Description | Dimensions | Quantity |
|------|-------------|------------|----------|
| A | Tall side | 1" x 4¾" x 10¼" | 1 |
| B | Short side | ¾" x 4¼" x 8¼" | 1 |
| C | Lower spacer | ⅞" x 2⅝" x 3½" | 1 |
| D | Middle spacer | ⅞" x 2⅝" x 3½" | 1 |
| E | Upper spacer | ⅜" x 2⅝" x 3½" | 1 |
| F | Drawer housing side | ⅜" x 2½" x 10" | 4 |
| G | Drawer | 1¾" x 1¾" x 5" | 2 |
| H | Drawer stop dowel | ¼" x ¾" | 2 |
| J | Detail, repeating assembly convex | ¼" x 1½" x 2½" | 3 |
| K | Detail, repeating assembly concave | ⅛" x 2" x 2½" | 6 |
| L | Detail, repeating assembly convex | ¼" x 1¼" x 1¾" | 1 |

- Use the tablesaw to prepare oversized blanks of contrasting woods for the complementary shapes of Part A and Part B, the tall and short sides. Mark out the shapes and bandsaw. Sand all faces to 220x. ▶

- Mill Part F, the drawer housing, from bocote or any available interesting wood. Parts are sized at twice the finished length; the resulting square tube will be crosscut to yield the two drawers. Sand the inside and outside faces of each part.

- Set the tablesaw at a 45 degree angle and rip a miter on the long edges of each of the four sides.

- Lay the four sides flat on the workbench, with long edges touching and miters facing down. Use masking tape to tape the parts together.

- Turn the entire taped assembly over and place a bead of glue in the trough formed by each pair of miters. (This technique is shown on page 80). Apply glue to the faces of the final two miters, and fold the assembly into a square tube. Use more tape to hold the final seam. Test the assembly for square.

- If glue has squeezed through to the inside surfaces of the tube, wait an hour or so until the glue has set, then carefully remove any excess with a sharp chisel.

- Use the tablesaw to crosscut the drawer housings to final size. Drill a ¼" hole in the top of each, ¼" back from the front edge, for the drawer-stop dowel. (After final assembly, this dowel will be hidden by Parts D and E, the spacers). Use the bandsaw to mill an angled score detail.

- Rough out Part G, the drawers, on the tablesaw as blocks of solid maple. Use a 1½" diameter flat-bottom bit to bore three overlapping holes in each block, creating the drawer cavity. (This process is illustrated on page 102).

- With a pencil and straight edge, mark out the crosshatch detail on the drawer fronts. Mill using the bandsaw.

- Flock the drawer interior using rayon powder flocking. With a small paintbrush, paint the interior surfaces of the drawer with latex paint the same color as the flocking material. Place the drawer and a quantity of flocking in a closed plastic container. Shake the container to distribute flocking evenly over the painted surface. When the paint is dry, clean up the top of the drawer by sanding it on the stationary belt sander, then gently blow out the excess.

- Insert the drawers, and install the drawer-stop dowels. The drawers can no longer be removed from their housings. Mill Parts C, D, and E, the three spacer blocks. ▶

- Lay Part A, the tall side, flat on the workbench and glue the drawer housings and spacers on its inside face. When dry, glue on Part B, the short side. ▼

- Mill Part K (repeating assembly, concave) and Parts J and L (repeating assembly, convex) from the same ¼" stock. After milling, bandsaw edge-notching and face-scoring details. Glue the repeating assembly and install. ▶

- Apply an oil finish, followed when dry by two coats of spray lacquer.

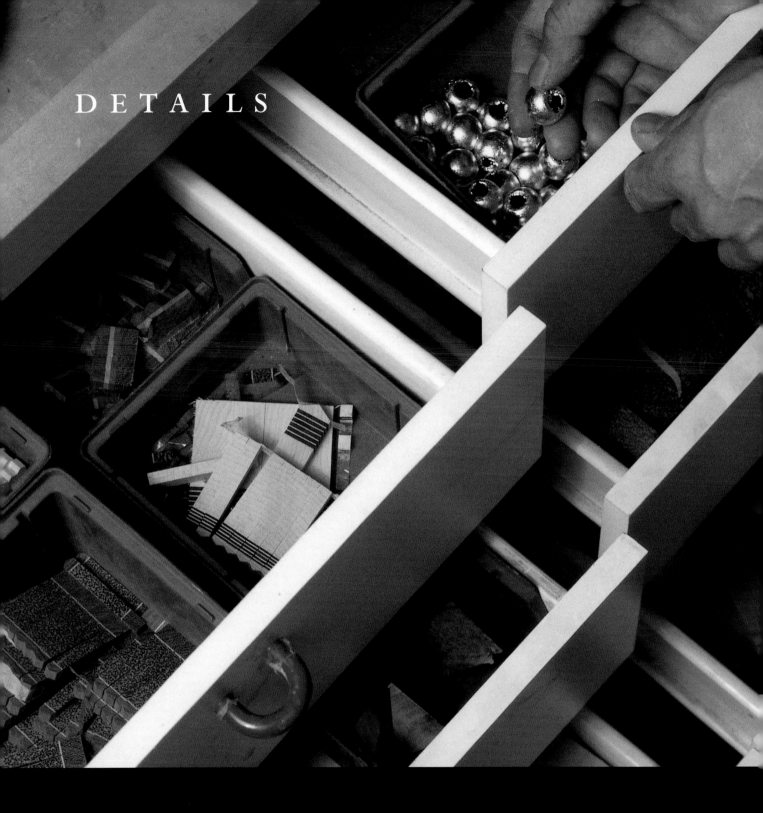

# DETAILS

The availability of neatly organized drawers filled with ready-made architectural details makes assembling a box design much easier. It also makes the process more fun, and stimulates the visual imagination, suggesting new shapes and combinations, and inviting unexpected design directions. Here are step by step instructions for making three of the details used in Po Shun's boxes: pyramids, obelisks and columns, and cones.

- Prepare 2" x 2" x 10" stock in as many woods as desired. Each will yield four square-base, four-sided pyramids 2" in height, plus eight narrower pyramids with one 90-degree base angle. Because of the difficulty of ripping short lengths on the table saw, make the stock a minimum of 10" long. ▶

- Set the blade of the tablesaw at a 20-degree angle, and rip. Tape the ripping back on and rip the other edge. ▶

- Set the miter fence to 60-degrees. The stock is now in three pieces: holding it firmly, crosscut as shown in the photograph. ▼

- Store completed pyramids in a parts drawer.

- On the table saw, mill stock in a variety of woods and dimensions, from ¾" x ¾" x 10" to 2" x 2" x 16". Because of the difficulty of ripping short lengths, make columns "two up", and crosscut after ripping.

- Use a pencil and straight edge to mark out profiles. For dark wood, wrap the stock with masking tape and draw on the tape. ▲

- Cut out the shapes on the bandsaw. ◀

- Obelisk shapes with extended flat surfaces may require sanding on the belt sander. ▶

- Store completed columns and obelisks in a parts drawer.

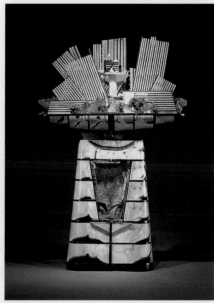

- To form each cone, a series of concentric circles, each bandsawed at a slight angle, are glued end to end. To get the hang of this technique, experiment with scrap softwood before proceeding to fine hardwood for the final project.

- Prepare stock for each cone as a solid block. This may be a single piece of wood, or a laminate of any type.

- With a compass, draw concentric circles on the face of the stock. ▶

- With the stock tilted at a 2-degree to 5-degree angle, cut through the side of the outer circle, then bandsaw it out of the block. Repeat this procedure for each concentric circle. ▶

- Glue each entry cut closed, using tape to clamp the seam until the glue dries. ▼

- Glue the concentric circles end to end to form a tapering cone, using tape to hold them until the glue dries. ▼

- When the cone is dry, sand the outer surface. ▲

# SAWDUST AND SHAVINGS

In Po Shun's workshop, no part of the tree goes unused. Many of the species that make up his boxes, such as the pink ivory wood shown here, yield brightly colored sawdust and shavings, which he uses to create sculptural collages. These small worlds invite the viewer to explore their mysterious inner spaces.

- To make a sawdust collage, start by building a four-sided box ¾" x 6" x 12". Use 45-degree miter joints, and make the back from a piece of ⅛" plywood glued into a ¼" deep sawkerf dado milled ⅛" in from the inside back edge of each side.

- Collect and store interesting sawdust and shavings, which will be applied to adhesive sprayed on selected surfaces of the collage. Several varieties of sawdust may be mixed together, but remember that in combination, colors may cancel each other out, producing a bland result.

- Inside the box, fabricate and glue an assortment of drawers, geometric and architectural elements. Drawers may be lined with flocking, and fitted with drawer-stop dowels. ▶

- Being careful not to let finishing materials touch the inner surfaces, apply an oil finish to the exterior of the collage. When the oil is dry, mask the interior and apply two coats of spray lacquer to the exterior.

- With tape, mask the edges of the box, the drawerfronts, and any other surfaces that are to be kept free of sawdust. Spray the remaining surfaces of the box interior and contents with spray adhesive. ▶

- Apply sawdust, shaking the box to make sure the sawdust is evenly distributed over the adhesive surface. Empty excess sawdust and clean. ▼

- For wall mounting, attach a mounting fixture to the back of the collage.

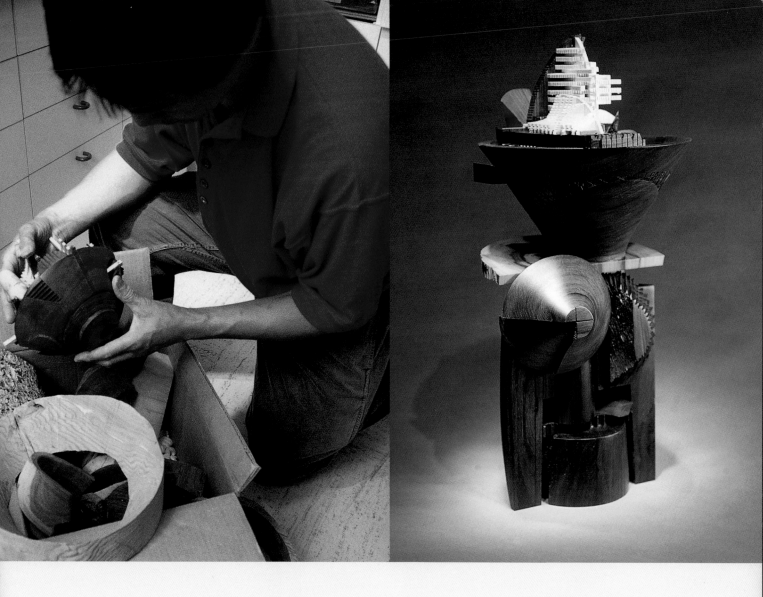

Years of networking have brought Po Shun the ultimate in recycling. Woodworking colleagues throughout the country send him their mistakes, breaks, failures, cutoffs and discards, which he promptly incorporates into his latest projects.

Shown here are materials contributed by Bob Stocksdale of California and Galen Carpenter of Arizona, two of the country's leading woodturners. Proceeds from the sale of pieces Po Shun makes from scrap are frequently donated to charity.

Another form of recycling involves incorporating elements from earlier projects into new designs. *Metropolis,* a freestanding triptych created in 1993, was disassembled to create the furniture on the opposite page.

The two left towers of *Metropolis* were used in the 1996 side table, above left. The third tower found its way into a set of coffee tables made in 1996, above right.

# LIST OF ILLUSTRATIONS IN GALLERY SECTION

Page 14
*Architectural Box*, 1987. 24″ x 18″ x 6″. Hawaiian Koa.
*Vase Shape Box*, 1988. 29″ x 18″ x 6″. Wenge.
*Box*, 1990. 12″ x 12″ x 6″. Buckeye Burl.

Page 15
*Tower Box*, 1988. 20″ x 10″ x 6″. Buckeye Burl.

Pages 16–17
*Cityscape Box*, 1993. 24″ x 21″ x 9″. Cherry burl & Maple.

Pages 18–19
*Twin Towers*, 1991. 36″ x 10″ x 6″. Pink Ivory Wood.
*Secret Places*, 1989. 30″ x 21″ x 10″. Pink Ivory Wood.

Page 20
*Tall Box*, 1993. 23″ x 20″ x 6″. Birds Eye Maple.

Page 21
*Rise and Fall*, 1992. 23″ x 18″ x 10″. Ash.
*Towers*, 1991. 30″ x 20″ x 6″. Maple.
*Black Landscape Box*, 1991. 22″ x 21″ x 9″. Stained Ash.
*Puzzle Box*, 1991. 30″ x 6″ x 6″. Various woods.

Pages 22–23
*Tall Box*, 1989. 72″ x 24″ x 14″. Buckeye Burl.
*Tall Box*, 1989. 72″ x 26″ x 15″. Cherry Burl.

Page 24
*Figure*, 1993. 51″ x 19″ x 10″. Mahogany.

Page 25
*Totem*, 1997. 72″ x 12″ x 15″. Various woods.

Page 26
*Pylon*, 1996. 30″ x 20″ x 6″. Maple & Wenge.

Page 27
*Up/Down*, 1993. 72″ x 9″ x 12″. Maple & Buckeye Burl.
*Tall Box*, 1994. 72″ x 24″ x 12″. Hawaiian Koa & Maple.
*Sculptural Box*, 1996. 96″ x 12″ x 15″. Mahogany.
*Totem Boxes*, 1997. 25″ x 11″ x 8″ & 24″ x 4″ x 4″. Various woods.

Page 28
*In Construction*, 1995. 25″ x 11″ x 8″. Bleached & stained Maple.

Page 29
*Figurative Box*, 1996. 32″ x 18″ x 12″. Wenge & Maple.

Page 30
*Box on Box*, 1994. 24″ x 18″ x 10″. Narra & Wenge.
*White on Black*, 1994. 24″ x 20″ x 8″. Wenge & Maple.

Page 31
*Modern Times*, 1994. 34″ x 23″ x 7″. Wenge & Maple.

Page 32
*Pendulum Box*, 1994. 36″ x 36″ x 6″. Pink Ivory wood & Wenge.

Page 33
*Cosmos Box*, 1994. 30″ x 24″ x 6″. Cherry Burl.

Pages 34–35
*Mask Boxes*, 1994. 36″ x 12″ x 8″. Narra.

Page 36
*Side Table*, 1990. 24″ x 20″ x 20″. Mahogany.
*Side Table*, 1990. 24″ x 18″ x 18″. Mahogany.
*Side Table*, 1996. 24″ x 18″ x 18″. Various woods.
*Side Table*, 1995. 24″ x 18″ x 18″. Bleached Wenge & Maple.

Page 37
*Side Table*, 1996. 24″ x 18″ x 18″. Mahogany.

Page 38
*Sit Down Dinner*, 1997. 47″ x 20″ x 18″. Wenge & Maple.

Page 39
*Set of 3 Coffee Tables*, 1996. 19″ x 30″ x 26″, 18″ x 30″ x 14″. Various.
*Coffee Table*, 1993. 18″ x 24″ x 30″. Various woods.

Pages 40–41
*Set of 2 Coffee Tables.*, 1996. 36″ x 38″ x 38″. Various woods.

Page 42
*Console Tables*, 1991, 1992, 1993, 1994, 1995, 1996, 1997. 36″ x 48″ x 16″. Various woods.

Page 43
*Console Table*, 1991. Detail. Various woods.

Pages 44–45
*Console Table*, 1997. 36″ x 52″ x 14″. Mahogany.

Pages 46–47
*Writing Desk & Chair*, 1996. 78″ x 39″ x 20″. Mahogany.

Page 48
*Pompeii Vessel #1*, 1989. 60″ x 14″ diameter. Mahogany.
*Pompeii Vessel: On Fire*, 1990. 60″ x 15″ x 15″. Pink Ivory Wood.

Page 49
*Pompeii Vessel: Chaos*, 1991. 60″ x 18″ x 18″. Various woods.
*Pompeii Vessel: Enclosure*, 1991. 60″ x 20″ x 12″. Mahogany.

Page 50
*Ark*, 1996. 20″ x 16″ x 16″. Bleached woods.
*Rocking Ark*, 1990. 60″ x 24″ x 12″. Wenge.
*Ark*, 1989. 18″ x 24″ x 9″. Buckeye Burl.
*Water World*, 1996. 24″ x 20″ x 7″. Mahogany.

Page 51
*Ark*, 1990. 18″ x 24″ x 9″. Buckeye Burl.

Page 52
*Warrior*, 1990. 24″ x 18″ x 6″. Buckeye Burl.

Page 53
*Figure*, 1993. 51″ x 19″ x 10″. Mahogany.

Page 54
*Mind over Matter*, 1990. 27″ x 18″ x 3″. Wood Collage.
*Kiln*, 1990. 27″ x 18″ x 3″. Wood Collage.

Pages 54–55
*The Rise and Fall of the City of Mahagonny*, 1990. 18″ x 54″ x 4″. Wood Collage.

Page 56
*Mesa Verde*, 1994. 55″ x 40″ x 9″. Various woods.

---

## PHOTO CREDITS

Page 11:   *Model of a Muhafiz Khan Mosque*, India, 1838. Wood. 57¼″ x 42¼″ x 33⅛″. Los Angeles County Museum Of Art, Ancient Art Council, British Gala Fund.
*Model of Tyringham House, Buckinghamshire*, England, 1793. Sir John Soane's Museum, London, England.

Page 12:   *Writing Cabinet*, India, Deccan, mid 17th century. Wood. 13″ x 22″ x 15″. Los Angeles County Museum of Art, Mr. and Mrs. Alan C. Balch Fund.
*Treasure Box Containing Thirty Items*, China. Ch'ing dynasty, Ch'ien-lung reign (1736-1795). Wood. 8¼″ x 9¾″ x 9⅝″. National Palace Museum, Taipei. Photograph by Bruce White.

James Cox. *Necessaire And Watch*, 1766-72. London. Agate, gold, pearls, paste, clockwork mechanism, carillon. 8¹¹⁄₁₆″ x 7½″ x 14⅛″. Arthur Gilbert Collection.

Page 13:   Naum Gabo. *Linear Construction in Space*, 1959. Aluminium and steel. 19″ x 13″ x 13″. Los Angeles County Museum of Art, Gift of Anna Bing Arnold.
Joseph Cornell. *Untitled, (Dovecote)*, ca 1950-54. Box construction, 10½″ x 7½″ x 4″; and *Untitled, (Compartmented Box)*, ca 1953. Box construction, 16¼″ x 11½″ x 2⅝″. Copyright, The Joseph and Robert Cornell Memorial Foundation. Courtesy C & M Arts.

# ACKNOWLEDGMENTS

I would like to thank the following individuals and organizations who have given invaluable help in the compilation of this book:

Jo Packham, President of Chapelle Ltd., who extended the invitation to do this book; Tony Lydgate, the author who made sense, created order and made his words feel like the images; Jo Lauria, Assistant Curator of Decorative Arts at the Los Angeles County Museum of Art, for putting it all into perspective; Richard Ader, Trustee of the Joseph and Robert Cornell Memorial Foundation, courtesy C & M Arts; Sir John Soane's Museum; Trustees of the Victoria and Albert Museum; National Palace Museum, Taipei; Arthur Gilbert Collection; and Leila Hadley, for her support and introduction to the works of Joseph Cornell.

Finally, a special thanks to the many people, some of whom are listed below who have given encouragement and enjoyed the art.

Norman & Phyllis Abramson
Gail Adams
Khaled Al-Awar
American Craft Council
American Craft Museum
Richard & Jana Anderson
James Anthony III
Jackie Bailey
Charles Barboni
Harvey & Jacqueline Barnett
Janet Baumgartner
Nicholas Beason
Mark Beaubien
Joanne Beck
Joseph & Lisa Becker
Pat Benetar
Beverly Benson
Reed & Lois Berger
Mitch & Linda Berliner
Alison Berman Hart
Kathleen Bette
Richard & Beth Binder
Gregory Binns
Neil Blake
Noyes & Susan Blankenbaker
Sally & Fred Blesi
Thomas Blount
Gorden Boyd
Larry & Deborah Brady
Peter Brandes
Bill & Wendy Braveman
Sidney & Phyllis Bresler
Deborah Bricker
Michael Brooks
Ellen Brout
Valeria Brown
Janet Brunelle
Dan Buckley
Maxine & Eric Burkholder
Edith & Lu Byerly
John Candy
Alan & Carol Caniglia
Thomas & Betty Carbol
Lynne Carmichael
Arthur Carota
David Carpenter
Galen & Ann Carpenter
Jim Carrey
Enrique Cervantes
Norvel & Joan Chan
Phyllis & Howard Cheskin
Sheldon & Lilly Chester
Bart & Linda Cirker
Dennis Christianson
John Christian
Rollin & Stephanie Christopherson
Ted & Ann Chronister
Fred Chu
John Cleese
Kathryn Cody
Arthur & Lynn Cohen
Ivan & Deborah Cohen
Ray & Marilyn Cohen
H Corbin Day
Judith & Stephen Corson
Zenaida Cosca
Theodore Craig- Smith
Vincent Crisci
Rebecca Cruz-Alvarez

Robert Culp
Jaime Davis
David & Maureen Doern
Ruth & Norman Don
Ann Donaldson
Richard & Mary Donnelley III
Addie Draper
Ann & Alfred Driscoll
Paul & Ceci Dry
Judy & Jerry Dubrof
Valerie Duff
Florence Duhl
Arthur & Norma Dunlop
William Dwyer
Alfred & Carol Edelman
Shirley Edidin
Susan Edson
Siegfried Ehrmann
Claes Elfing
Lawrence Elliman
Jerome & Deborah Epstein
Sara Epstein
Marjorie Erdman
Linda Evans
John & Dolores Eyler
Penelope Farley
William & Barbara Felton
Janice Ferri
Jerry Fiddler
Lynn Fischcher
Julian & Barbara Fisher
Guy Fishman
Roger & Diane Fishman
Dolly Fiterman
P & D Fitzsimmons
Victor Fong
Charles Forni III
Ed Frank
Mary Frederick
David & Wendy Fretzin
Rhoda Friedman
True Given
Patricia Gilman
Alan Gleitsman
Whoppi Goldberg
Bruce & Michelle Golden
Peter & Sandra Gorski
Betty & Harry Gottlieb
Susie & Bob Grey
Richard & Mary Greenwalt
Eric & Ellie Greenberg
Martha Greenberg
Joanne Griese
Barry & Erica Gudelsky
Nancy Hale
Andrea Hanaway
Paul Harrington
Marylou Hartmann
Lorraine Heinichen
Leila & Henry Luce III
Carol & William Henwood
Lloyd Herman
Janet Hertherington
Norma Hoffman
Alice Homer
Sean Hooper
Irwin Horwitch
Kathryn Hughes
Dean & April Huspen

Lori & Hilton Hyland
Harold & Rita Tooby
Charlene & Paul Johnson
Dan & Den Jones
Neil Kamin
Jeffrey Kaplan
Laura Karp
A & Faith Kash
Laura Katz
Alice Kawazoe
Doris Keever
Jacqueline Kellog
Richard & Deborah Kendall
Sharon Kent
Robert & Eulalia Klaus
Nancy & Richard Klavens
Rebecca Klemm
Joan Kling
Ellen Kochansky
Timothy & Sheryl Kochman
Marvin & Edna Korengold
Jane Korman
Frederic Kremer
Nan Laitman
John Lamb
Robert & Linda Lane
Bud Laven
Jo Lauria
Le Corbusier
June Lefkovitz
Alexander & Marianne Lerner
Irvin & Mary Lipton
Harvey Listz
David & Jennifer Liu
Florence Lo Patin
Judith London Newton
Fidel Lopez
Lester & Ruth Luborsky
Camille Marker
Steve Martin
George Maslach
Jane & Arthur Mason
Agnesann Mathis
Gayle Maxon
Patricia McKinnon
Andrew & Lester McCarthy
Patricia McCauley
Thomas McCorreston
Bruce McIntyre
Patricia McKeon
Susanne McLean
Robert & Lorel McMillan
Rita Meltzer
Evan Mendelson
Paul Meyer
Joseph & Jennifer Meyerhoff II
Ilene Miller
Jeffrey Miller
Toby Mills
Minnesota Museum of
   American Art
Alan Mintz
John Moag Jr.
Lynn Moffic
Alan Molod
Michael Monroe
Ann Morales
Keven Moran
Frances Morgan

Martha Morris
Ed Mouthrop
Greg & Catherine Muldowney
Martina Navritolova
Edward & Jennifer Nazarko
Ruth Nelson
Timothy Newton
Marion Nord
Carol North
Thomas & Nancy o'Connor
Judith & Ike Oberman
Linda Olup
Grace Ong Hing
Stuart Opotowsky
Diana Pappas
Penny Parker
Von & Ruth Peacock
Dennis & Constance Petertson
Greg & Susan Pfaff
Philadelphia Museum of Art
Barbara Pollock
Charles & Edith Poor
Carol Port
Larry Pozner
Joe Price
Fred & Judy Prillaman
Ida Prosky
Kathleen Randall
Ray & Jennifer Redd
Robert Reilert
Renwick Gallery
Gretchen Rhodes
Austra Richards
Michael & Phyllis Robertson
Barbara Robertson
Joseph & Joan Roebuck
Kenneth & Mary Roffe
Lester & Deborah Rosen
Arnold & Gail Rosenthal
Bernard & Barbara Rothschild
Mary Rowell
Herbert Rozoff
Shirley & Howard Rubin
David & Catherine Ruef
Martin & Sigrid Rutstein
Carol Safer
Colgate & Rhea Salsbury
Charles Samer
Kevin Saunders
Arthur Sawl
Ira Scharfglass
Carol Schilling
Sandra Schlachtmeyer
Darlene Schmalzried
Judith Schmidt
Joan Schneider
Patricia & Maurice Schwartzmann
Marcia Seidletz
Jacqueline & Howard Shapiro
Roger Shapiro
Arti Shaw
Susan Shipper Smith
Diane Shuck
Harriet Siegal
Dianne Sickmann
Mike Silver
Edward Silver
Robert & Sandra Silver
David Slainger

Smithsonian Institution
Mary Smotrys
Robert Snyder
Harry & Branka Sondheim
Jayne Sonnenschein
Alfonso & Julietta Soto Soria
Karen & Joseph Steger
Cheryl Stein
Sydney & Bertha Stein
Susan Steinberg
Philip Stern
Regina Stillinger
Bob Stocksdale
Frances & Harry Stover
Francine Strauss
Mary & Frank Strawbridge
Keith Stroup
Arlene Sunkel
Sidney Sussman
Douglas Tannett
Kit Taylor
Sara Thiermann
Samuel Todes
Neil & Sheila Tuber
Roslyn Tunis
Scott Turow
Linda Univerzagt
Howard & Maralyn Usen
Ronald Veasley
Daniel Viers
Cathleen Wadhams
Irene Wagner
Barbara Waldman
Ann Day Wallick
Charles & Laurie Wang
Kent Watkins
Paul & Shirley Weber
Paul & Harriet Weinberg
Paul Weston
White House Craft Collection
Robin Williams
Charles A Wustum Museum
Yale University Art Gallery
Sharon Young
Julia & Isiah Zagar
Susan Zimicki
Hank & Lisa Zucker
And special thanks to:
Brigitte Jodexnis
Hans-Juergen Kraushaar

# METRIC CONVERSION CHART

| inches | mm | cm | inches | cm | inches | cm |
|--------|-----|------|--------|------|--------|--------|
| ⅛ | 3 | 0.3 | 11 | 27.9 | 33 | 83.8 |
| ¼ | 6 | 0.6 | 12 | 30.5 | 34 | 86.4 |
| ⅜ | 10 | 1.0 | 13 | 33.0 | 35 | 88.9 |
| ½ | 13 | 1.3 | 14 | 35.6 | 36 | 91.4 |
| ⅝ | 16 | 1.6 | 15 | 38.1 | 37 | 94.0 |
| ¾ | 19 | 1.9 | 16 | 40.6 | 38 | 96.5 |
| ⅞ | 22 | 2.2 | 17 | 43.2 | 39 | 99.1 |
| 1 | 25 | 2.5 | 18 | 45.7 | 40 | 101.6 |
| 1¼ | 32 | 3.2 | 19 | 48.3 | 41 | 104.1 |
| 1½ | 38 | 3.8 | 20 | 50.8 | 42 | 106.7 |
| 2 | 51 | 5.1 | 21 | 53.3 | 43 | 109.2 |
| 2½ | 64 | 6.4 | 22 | 55.9 | 44 | 111.8 |
| 3 | 76 | 7.6 | 23 | 58.4 | 45 | 114.3 |
| 3½ | 89 | 8.9 | 24 | 61.0 | 46 | 116.8 |
| 4 | 102 | 10.2 | 25 | 63.5 | 47 | 119.4 |
| 4½ | 114 | 11.4 | 26 | 66.0 | 48 | 121.9 |
| 5 | 127 | 12.7 | 27 | 68.6 | 49 | 124.5 |
| 6 | 152 | 15.2 | 28 | 71.1 | 50 | 127.0 |
| 7 | 178 | 17.8 | 29 | 73.7 | | |
| 8 | 203 | 20.3 | 30 | 76.2 | | |
| 9 | 229 | 22.9 | 31 | 78.7 | | |
| 10 | 254 | 25.4 | 32 | 81.3 | | |

# INDEX